I0518804

HEROINE

DECIDE & CONQUER

BY CHASTIDY MADER

© 2026 Chastidy Mader

Interior Book Design & Formatting: DNP Presents

ALL RIGHTS RESERVED. No part of this book may be reproduced in any written, electronic, recording, or photocopying without the written permission of the publisher or author. The exception would be in the case of brief quotations embodied in critical articles or reviews and pages where permission is specifically granted by the publisher or author.

LEGAL DISCLAIMER. Although the author has made every effort to ensure that the information in this book was correct at press time, the author does not assume, hereby disclaim any liability to any party for loss, damage, or disruption caused by errors or omissions, whether such errors or omissions result from negligence, accident, or any other cause.

Published By: DNP Presents a Veritas Publishing House Imprint

Library of Congress Cataloging-in-Publication Data has been applied for

ISBN: 979-8-9934977-0-9

PRINTED IN THE UNITED STATES OF AMERICA

Epigraph:

Heroine.

It's a word that holds two truths in my life.

One is a woman of courage — someone who fights her way back from darkness, battles demons, and stands in the light for others to see.

The other is the drug that nearly destroyed me — that seduced me, silenced me, and stole everything I thought I was.

This story is about both.

Because I was both.

But only one of them gets to write the ending.

— Chastidy Mader

Prologue – The Lanterns

I always admired the blown-glass lamps of the Alexander Hotel. They shone brightly, especially around twilight, when Levi and I would drive past on our way into the city, surely exhausted from our last drug-fueled endeavor. I'd picture him in a suit and tie, me in an elegant dress, as we walked through its doors for some beautiful reason — a special occasion, a night that meant something. But we never had one.

The lamps hung like firelit jewels in the second-floor dining room — glowing in shades of orange, blue, yellow, purple, and green. I loved the way the colors clashed and harmonized, like stained glass suspended midair. Maybe once, I could've passed for someone who belonged there. But Levi and I? We were from a different world. A different class — if you could even call it that.

Still, every time we passed the hotel, I'd look. And dream. Maybe one day, in some better version of my life, I'd finally have a reason to step inside.

Table of Contents

No Longer Hiding

For a long time, I believed that staying quiet was the safest choice. I told myself it was professional, responsible, protective. I thought that if I worked hard enough, rebuilt carefully enough, and kept my past neatly contained, I could move forward without ever having to name where I had been. Silence felt like control. Distance felt like safety.

But silence has a cost.

I wrote Heroine: Decide & Conquer during a time when survival came before visibility. The book was never written to shock or provoke. It was written because I needed to tell the truth somewhere — even if that truth lived only on the page. At the time, anonymity felt necessary. I was still rebuilding my life, my career, and my sense of self. I believed that staying hidden was the price of being allowed to move on.

What I didn't realize then was that hiding slowly became another form of confinement.

Over time, as my life stabilized and my work deepened, the distance between who I was publicly and what I had lived privately began to feel dishonest — not in a dramatic way, but in a quiet, exhausting one. I found myself helping others navigate addiction, recovery, shame, and rebuilding while keeping my own story carefully out of view. I could offer compassion, structure, and guidance — but only up to a certain point. There was an invisible line I would not cross, and I felt it every time someone looked at me and wondered if I truly understood.

The truth is simple: I cannot help people fully while hiding my face.

Recovery is not built on perfection. It is built on honesty, accountability, and the willingness to be seen — not as flawless, but as real. The more work I did in my own healing, the clearer it became that the very thing I was protecting myself from was the thing that allowed others to trust me. My silence was not neutral. It created distance where connection was needed.

I also came to understand that hiding implied something I no longer believe: that my past disqualified me from credibility instead of grounding it.

I am not ashamed of the work it took to get here. I am not ashamed of recovery. I am not ashamed of having struggled inside a system that often demands endless strength without adequate support — especially from those in caregiving roles. What once felt like a liability is, in reality, part of my authority. I know this terrain because I lived it.

At a certain point, continuing to hide stopped being about protection and started being about fear — fear of judgment, fear of misunderstanding, fear of being reduced to a chapter of my life instead of the whole of it. But fear is not a sustainable foundation for a life built on service. And it is not a value I want to model for the people I hope to help.

There is also this truth: I no longer have a reason to hide.

I have done the work. I have taken responsibility. I have rebuilt with intention. My life today is not fragile, and my story is not finished. I am not asking for absolution or permission. I am standing in ownership.

Hiding once felt like humility. Now it feels like erasure.

Coming forward as the author of Heroine: Decide & Conquer is not about revisiting the past for its own sake. It is about integration. It is about allowing all parts of my story — the difficult ones and the hard-won ones — to exist in the same light. It is about refusing to live split between who I was and who I am.

I am tired of hiding — not because hiding is weak, but because I am no longer willing to live small to make others comfortable. I am tired of carefully editing myself to fit into spaces that benefit from my insight while pretending it came from somewhere abstract. My experience is not theoretical. It is lived. And it has value.

This decision is also an act of advocacy.

There are countless professionals — especially women and healthcare workers — who are quietly struggling under the weight of expectation, stigma, and silence. Many believe that if their truth were known, they would lose everything. I once believed that too. By standing openly in my story now, I hope to expand the space for honesty and reduce the shame that keeps so many people suffering in silence.

Visibility is not about attention. It is about permission.

Permission to ask for help sooner. Permission to recover without disappearing. Permission to understand that competence and struggle can coexist in the same person — and often do.

I am not coming forward to be defined by addiction. I am coming forward because recovery has shaped my integrity, my work, and my purpose. I am not interested in being admired for surviving. I am interested in being useful to those who are still finding their way.

I can no longer ask people to be brave while remaining hidden myself.

So, this is me, showing my face — not as a confession, not as a spectacle, but as a declaration that my story belongs to me. I choose to stand in it fully, without apology or secrecy, and to let it serve something larger than fear.

This is not the end of my story. It is the point where I stopped hiding from it.

Chastidy Mader

Part 1:

The Descent

Chapter 1

Toehead in the Hands of God

I was a sweet child — I really was. I must have been quite cute, too; I was always called "Blue Eyes" or "Dimples." I was a little "toehead," as they say. My hair was almost white-blonde, and my eyes were the color of cornflowers. To top it off, the dimples in both my cheeks formed little valleys whenever I smiled.

I was happy-go-lucky and made friends easily. I often gravitated toward kids who seemed shy or lonely. It wasn't enough for me to just wave and walk past; something in me wanted to sit with them, ask questions, and figure out why they seemed so sad. Even then, it felt like I had a mission—to bring joy and friendship into lives where there wasn't much of either.

Looking back now, maybe this was the first sign of where my path would eventually lead—for both the bad and the good.

I'll never forget one still, quiet Sunday morning. The house seemed unusually peaceful, as if even the air didn't want to stir. How I even knew it was Sunday, I don't remember. I couldn't have been older than eight. But the memory is as clear as if it happened yesterday.

I woke up with a strange sense of invitation—an unspoken nudge, like someone had tapped on my shoulder and whispered, *"Come with Me."* There wasn't a sound in the house, yet I felt certain someone had knocked on my bedroom door and asked me to go to church. By whom, I had no idea.

I crossed the hall on tiptoe and tapped gently on my mother's door.

"Mom? Can I go to church today?" I asked softly, almost afraid she'd say no.

"Sure, sweetie. Just be careful on your way there," she said, her voice muffled but warm.

Before I knew it, I was dressed in my only Sunday best—a purple floral dress with a lace collar—and headed to the little church just two blocks away.

It was that day I met the woman I would come to know as my spiritual mother for the rest of my life.

"Who are you with, honey?" she asked, flashing the biggest, sweetest smile I'd ever seen. Her short blonde curls bounced as she chomped her gum. There was something magnetic about her—a joy that felt contagious. I liked her immediately.

"Nobody," I replied, suddenly aware of how alone I must have looked.

"Well, God love you! Bless your sweet little heart," she said, her voice lilting and full of warmth. She reached into her handbag and handed me a bite-sized candy bar. *"Come with me. I'll show you where to go."*

She led me to the Sunday school room, her perfume – a comforting mix of powder and flowers. From then on, my life was never the same.

To this day, whenever I think about walking to that church, I never see myself alone. In my mind's eye, the view is always from behind—of my little self, walking hand in hand with Jesus, with Him on the street side (He is a gentleman, after all).

I wore my purple floral dress. He wore the whitest robe, a sash draped over His shoulder, and sandals that left faint impressions on the dusty sidewalk. His hair was shoulder-length and brown, swaying gently with each step.

Now that I write this, it makes sense that the image in my memory shows Him from behind. The Bible says no one can behold the face of God because He is so holy that it would be fatal.

My spiritual mother wasted no time telling me about the precious sacrifice Jesus made for me. She spoke with such conviction, as if she could see the weight of the world waiting on my little shoulders. I accepted Him quickly and wholeheartedly, my childlike heart wide open.

And thank God I did.

The road ahead was daunting and not for the faint of heart. He knew I would need Him sooner rather than later. He also knew I'd be a tough one to convince as I got older, so He invited me while I was still young, impressionable, and receptive.

As I moved through grade school, I may as well have been a little missionary. I prayed for others, led my friends to Christ, and took my relationship with God seriously.

It wasn't until my teenage years that I began to rebel—and even that started from an innocent place. I befriended a girl caught in her own battles. Her parents had separated and were getting divorced. At first, I tried to be a good influence. But over time, I gave in to the temptation of peer pressure.

It didn't help that I had the biggest crush on her older brother. He was a couple of years older and—oh, so cute. I wanted more than anything to be accepted, to seem cool in their eyes.

Looking back now, I realize there was nothing I could have done to earn their acceptance. But at that age, you don't know that yet.

Chapter 2:

A Whole New World

I had my daughter, Mary, at sixteen. I named her after my grandmother, hoping she would carry forward something of the strength and grace I'd seen in her.

Mary was due in September 2001, but she came two weeks early. On August 26, 2001, I became a mother.

It's funny: as I lay alone in a strange hospital room, in labor, I remember thinking, *I hope there's nothing crazy going on in the world today.*

Even now, I can't explain why that thought crossed my mind. Before that day, I'd always been lost in my own little world—half-dreaming, half-hustling, too busy trying to grow up too fast.

At sixteen, I thought becoming a teen mom would catapult me straight into adulthood, like flipping a switch. I couldn't have been more wrong.

As far back as I can remember, I've been in a rush— always reaching for the next thing, convinced that if I could just get there, I'd finally feel whole. 2001 was no different.

The pregnancy had interrupted my path to an honors diploma, one I thought would be my ticket out of poverty and the narrow future I'd grown up believing was all there was for me. I was furious at myself for derailing my plans.

I've always had the tools to succeed—but I haven't always known how to use them right. Even back in junior high, I partied on weekends but still made straight A's. I was on the cheer squad, and in eighth grade, I even earned the coveted citizenship award, along with a sponsorship to participate in varsity sports once I got to Bloomington South.

Two weeks after Mary's birth—on her actual due date—I left her with her father, Leroy, and went back to pursue my high school diploma. *Come hell or high water*, I told myself, *I am not settling for a life of mediocrity.*

That morning, I walked into my first class, a computer lab during first period. I felt fat and out of place in my too-tight clothes. The smell of pencil shavings and dry-erase markers hit me, and I caught sight of my reflection in the dark monitor screen. For a second, I didn't recognize the tired, wary girl looking back.

It didn't take long to realize I'd outgrown the antics of teenage-dom. Not intentionally—just circumstantially.

When the first-period bell rang, I felt more relief than I expected, like my lungs had been holding onto stale air. Little did I know, I was about to step into a moment that would change my life's trajectory forever.

As I walked the tile hallway toward my next class, I passed the auditorium. A television mounted high on the wall caught my eye. Smoke was pouring from the side of a tall building.

Ashamed as I am to admit it, my first thought was, *I wonder what war-torn country is being bombed this time.*

Maybe I said it out loud, or maybe my face betrayed my indifference. Because what I heard next stopped me cold.

"That's not in another country," a student said flatly. *"That's New York City. A plane just crashed into one of the Twin Towers."*

For the first time in my life, I felt fear so intense it made me want to vomit.

Right then, I decided I wasn't staying. A few friends I'd made prior to school agreed to leave too, and they gave me a ride home. I didn't even have a driver's license yet.

When I got home, I turned on the television. My heart sank. A second plane had crashed into the other Twin Tower.

A sense of urgency flooded me. I didn't have words for it, but I knew we were in trouble. I knew my life as I'd known it was over and the time for innocence and youth had come to a screeching halt. It was time to grow up right now—but yesterday would've been better.

The next thing I remember is preparing for GED classes. I did it solely so I could apply for nursing school. Honestly, I don't even remember deciding on nursing; it just... happened. It felt like the only option, the next step in the rush to get my life together.

I think the decision was layered. Nursing would allow me to contribute meaningfully to my country while providing for myself and my daughter. I even spoke to a Navy recruiter once, but I wasn't old enough for the military. That door wasn't open, but I wanted my boots on the ground now. I was convinced the draft would return, and I couldn't shake the thought that my boyfriend would be chosen—and not come back.

To say I was in fight-or-flight mode would be an understatement. I carried that energy through all of nursing school—and maybe I still do today.

The next few months passed in a blur of late nights, early mornings, and constant studying. Before I knew it, I was enrolled in prerequisite classes for the nursing program.

I'll never forget the heartbreak I felt the first day of class—Anatomy & Physiology. It was August 26, 2002.

Mary's first birthday.

My heart ached as I dropped her off at daycare for the first time. She was way too young. I can still see her in those tiny jean overalls with the heart-shaped pocket and little bell-bottoms. Her golden strawberry-blonde hair framed her baby face as she toddled off with the teacher, clutching her bunny like it was an anchor in a storm.

I worried sick all morning. At lunch, I visited her classroom. There she was, sitting at a tiny table with her peers, eating the lunch I'd packed for her the night before.

From the very beginning, she was a victim of my constant rushing. And 9/11 hadn't slowed me down—it had only fueled my urgency.

I'll forever be grateful she was born two weeks early. I wouldn't have wanted her birthday tied to such a traumatic day in history.

Her entire life, she was forced to start things before she was ready. She came into the world early, started daycare on her first birthday, started "school" at K3 when she was two, and on it went.

Being young made me a less-than-worthy mother. I want to say I did the best I could all those years, but I still wonder: *Did I really?*

They say hindsight is 20/20. Looking back, I see how often I chose profession and position over being a present mother. I believe I'll carry that regret with me forever.

The truth is, I didn't understand the responsibility of raising another human being—or the weight it carried.

I often yearned for more nurturing myself, so maybe I didn't know how to give what I'd never received. But hear me: I'm not saying my mother didn't give me all she could. She endured worse circumstances in her life than I ever did.

Today, I grieve for her—the child and young woman she was. Had she gotten what she needed back then, I'm certain I'd be a neurosurgeon today.

Even with the limited love and nurturing she was able to give me, I still became resilient—and even, successful.

Chapter 3:

Flash of Blood

Nursing school felt like what I was made for.

When I started classes, I was only seventeen—the youngest in my cohort by far. But instead of shrinking back, I rose to the challenge. In a way, I felt like I had something to prove—not just to the world but to myself.

Even so, I was surprised at how quickly I rose to the top. Concepts that seemed daunting at first began to click. I could almost feel my brain reawakening, firing on all cylinders. Soon, I was tutoring other students, explaining material in a way that made their faces light up with understanding. For the first time in a long time, I felt like I wasn't failing at life.

Each milestone became a little victory, stacking up like bricks under my feet, lifting me higher. Making the Dean's List repeatedly was like a drumbeat of validation: *See? You're not broken. You're capable. You belong here.* When I was offered a scholarship, it felt like the universe itself was whispering, *Keep going. You're on the right track.*

After completing my prerequisites and entering the nursing program, I chose the practical nursing track, where the true testing would begin. It was shorter and would allow me to start working sooner. I told myself, *This isn't the end. It's just the first step.*

During that program, I didn't just keep pace; I thrived. I served as our class president and was even chosen to be the class speaker for graduation. Standing at that podium, my hands shaking slightly around the edges of my speech, I felt something I hadn't felt in years: pride that wasn't tinged with shame.

It was as if I were finally picking up where I'd left off before my teenage pregnancy had knocked me off course.

Not long after graduation, my school offered a transition track for becoming a registered nurse. Only ten students would be selected. The odds were stacked against me, but when I received my acceptance letter, I was stunned. My hands trembled as I read it over and over, almost not daring to believe it was real. I was elated.

Six months into my nursing career, I was back in school again, hungry for more. It was as if a dam had broken, and now there was no stopping the flow.

Through all my stumbles in those early years, I had still managed to become an LPN by nineteen and an RN by twenty-one.

I felt on top of the world.

But if I'm honest, I wasn't ready.

I was too young, too traumatized, and too naïve for what I was about to step into. Nursing isn't just a career; it's a front-row seat to life and death, hope and heartbreak, triumph and tragedy—and I was still figuring out how to navigate my own pain.

Still, I had no choice. So, I pressed forward into a big, scary, unforgiving world. Though I was afraid, I kept pushing.

Little victories built my confidence: starting my first IV, seeing that telltale flash of blood in the catheter chamber, and feeling that quiet thrill of success wash over me. It wasn't just pride—it was relief, gratitude, and a spark of something I couldn't quite name.

That *"blood flash"* became a reward system in my brain. Every time I saw it, I felt a rush—like I was leveling up, proving my worth.

Later, I would realize that this same part of me—the one hungry for that rush—would awaken something far more sinister.

Still, at that time, I believed there was greatness in me—something bigger than myself, something meant for more.

Chapter 4:

Picturesque

*E*ach day I took steps forward, though sometimes it felt like I was taking two steps back.

During my early nursing years, I married my high school boyfriend, Mary's father.

From the moment I met him, I was smitten. He was older, drove a brand-new cherry-red truck, and had ice-blue eyes set against dark hair. There was an effortless coolness about him that drew me in like a magnet. I found him irresistible.

He was the teacher's aide in my class, and I've always been drawn to people with quiet power. He and his best friend were the senior guys everyone seemed to part ways for in the hallways, like the Red Sea. They didn't speak loudly or draw attention on purpose—it was just something in the way they carried themselves.

And I wanted to be part of that.

I was tired of being the quiet, shy girl. Tired of being bullied and overlooked. When he noticed me, it felt like a door opening to a world I wasn't sure I deserved to step into.

And just like that, that chapter of my life ended.

Our wedding was nothing short of picturesque. It was held in the country, on a beautiful piece of land where wildflowers dotted the fields and the breeze carried the faint scent of honeysuckle.

In nursing school, I'd befriended a woman who—unbeknownst to me—owned a bridal shop that was closing as she pursued her own career in nursing.

Not only was everything 75% off (or more), but she also gifted me many items for the ceremony. Her generosity felt like a blessing straight from God, like He was saying, *This is for you, child. I see you.*

I found the most beautiful white gown, and it's true what they say: you just know when you put on *the one.*

Another friend from the practical nursing program, Wendy, had become my best friend and stood by me as my maid of honor. I felt blessed to have these women in my life—kind souls who believed in me when I barely believed in myself.

The gown was a halter-top style with intricate beading across the bodice. It had a detachable embroidered train that revealed layers of extravagant lace underneath. My veil sparkled with mother-of-pearl beads woven through a tiara-like headpiece.

I wore satin gloves as I walked down the aisle to my groom.

In that moment, I felt like Cinderella after her fairy godmother had waved her wand.

It was perfect.

Looking back now, I don't think I realized how blessed I was to have been given so much for that day. I didn't have the words for it then, but I felt wrapped in a kind of grace I couldn't explain.

And I'm still grateful for the friends who poured into me during that time, stitching joy and beauty into a season when I desperately needed it.

Chapter 5:

Crisscross Applesauce

I was married to that man for a long time, and together we had three beautiful children.

Mary was our first blessing. From the moment I knew she was coming, she began to change my life for the better.

I remember being alone in my hospital room after she was born. Maybe it was because I was so young, but the nurses seemed to assume I didn't care whether my baby was with me.

They couldn't have been more wrong.

I waited as patiently as I could, staring at the clock on the wall, listening to the faint squeak of nurses' shoes on the linoleum floor outside. But after about four hours, I couldn't take it anymore. I finally ventured out of my room in my hospital gown and socks, my hair pulled back in a messy knot.

I tiptoed down the hall toward the nursery, my heart pounding with a mix of excitement and anxiety.

It's funny how all babies seem to look alike—until one of them is yours.

I spotted her instantly. She had a tiny oxygen mask over her face, and my heart broke.

"Can I please have my baby now?" I asked the nurses, my voice soft but firm.

They walked over, checked her oxygen levels, and—almost reluctantly—handed her to me.

Before I knew it, she and I were back in my room.

I held that little miracle in my arms, breathing in her warm, powdery scent, feeling her tiny chest rise and fall against me. I felt more love than I ever thought possible.

I remember thinking, *I will never be alone again.*

She lay on my belly in the same position she had been in just twelve hours earlier, inside of me. Her little legs were crossed and drawn up—reminding me of sitting crisscross applesauce (though we didn't call it that when I was a child).

I patted her diapered bottom and whispered, *"Don't worry. We'll always have each other."*

Again, I thanked God that we didn't have to share her birthday with the tragedies of 9/11. I needed that day to be just ours—and so it was.

Our next pregnancy went much smoother. By then, we were married. I'd been practicing nursing for about three years and felt more secure in life. I was working on a busy ortho-neuro unit as a registered nurse, I was a wife, and for the first time, I felt accomplished and confident.

But that confidence didn't last long.

The next trauma was already looming—like the reaper of joy, waiting just around the corner.

Chapter 6:

Boiling Water

By then, I was working what we in healthcare call "weekend option." I was also working nights.

There were good reasons for that schedule. For one, I was hugely pregnant, my feet hurt constantly, and, truthfully, I was exhausted in a way only other mothers could understand. Working nights allowed me to do two twelve-hour shifts instead of three while still being paid for three. It was less grueling and chaotic, allowing me to spend more time with Mary during the week.

I took her to and from school, cooked dinner, cleaned the house—I felt like I was doing it all.

But I still remember the day it all began to unravel.

It was around 3:15 in the afternoon. The house was quiet except for the soft bubbling of water on the stove. I was cooking spaghetti for dinner, letting the pot heat as I walked down the driveway to check the mail like I did every other day.

The sunlight was warm against my skin, but I felt heavy—my belly stretching the gray maternity dress I had thrown on that morning. My flip-flops slapped against the concrete as I bent down to pull the stack of envelopes from the box.

As I flipped through the pile, one caught my eye: a paper cell phone bill.

We'd gone paperless months ago.

I frowned. It felt thicker than usual—too thick.

Something in my stomach tightened.

I ripped it open right there, standing in the driveway, scanning the pages for anything out of place.

And then I saw it.

A record of texts, calls, and multimedia messages. One phone number kept appearing over and over again, at all hours of the day and night.

The number wasn't familiar. But the area code was.

Standing there, holding that bill in my hand, I felt dizzy. My pregnant belly felt impossibly heavy. My mind began to race. *Whose number is this? Why don't I recognize it?*

3:28 PM.

My husband always got off work at 3:30. Every single day, like clockwork, he called me as soon as he left.

But now I saw it: calls to this other number at 3:28, 3:29—right before he called me.

My heart pounded in my ears. A sick, twisting feeling settled in my gut. I couldn't wait another second.

I dialed the number with trembling hands.

No answer. But then came the voicemail.

"Hey, this is Sarah. Leave me a message!"

Her voice was twangy, unfamiliar.

The world seemed to tilt beneath me. I thought I might pass out right there in the kitchen.

The water on the stove had started boiling.

I needed him home—now.

Thank God it was just before he got off work. I couldn't handle waiting any longer for answers.

I called him before he had a chance to contact me.

The phone rang once. Twice.

"Hello?" he said, his voice calm, as if nothing was amiss.

The words flew out of my mouth before I could stop them.

"Whose number is on our phone bill? The one that's in contact with you more than I am? The one you're calling at all hours. I called it. It's a woman. You need to get home. Right now."

There was silence on the other end of the line.

To me, that betrayal felt as traumatic as 9/11—except this time it was personal.

When he walked through the door minutes later, I was waiting. My face was hot with anger, my hands gripping the paper bill so tightly it crumpled in my fist.

"Give me your phone," I demanded.

He hesitated, then handed it over, and I dialed her number.

"Hello?" she answered.

"Why are you always talking to my husband?" I snapped.

She froze. I could hear her struggling to speak.

My husband took over the conversation. *"I told her we're just friends,"* he said.

The call was on speakerphone. I needed to hear every word.

The conversation was short. She agreed there was nothing going on between them, that they were "just friends."

But in my gut, I knew the truth.

Still, I was six months pregnant with our second daughter, Annie. I told myself I had to let it go. I wanted to believe him. I tried to believe him.

But deep down, I knew I was missing something.

Chapter 7:

Missing Something

*I*t's strange, the things a person will believe when they really want—or need—to.

After that day, my husband swore time and again that he and Sarah were "just friends."

I wanted to believe him. God knows I wanted to.

But my gut gnawed at me like a slow, deep hunger that wouldn't go away.

At night, lying awake in the dark beside him, I'd hear the faint buzz of his phone on the nightstand. I'd force myself to stay still, to not lift my head to peer over at his phone screen. My thoughts swirled like water circling a drain: *What if I'm wrong? What if I'm right?*

I didn't have time to dig deeper. Annie was due in a couple of months, and I had to focus on keeping myself calm and preparing for her arrival. Stress wasn't good for the baby—I knew that. So, I buried it.

I forced myself to move on, to pretend it had been nothing, to convince myself I was overreacting—that maybe I had misconstrued the whole thing.

But deep down, I knew.

I was missing something.

Chapter 8:

Baby Doll

*T*hankfully, after that incident, my husband and I grew closer again.

We spent time preparing Annie's nursery, carefully folding soft baby blankets, listening to good music on discs we'd burned of our favorites, and taking long drives to pass the time. There were moments when it almost felt like we were back to the way things had been—before suspicion crept in and settled like dust on every surface.

Before we knew it, induction day arrived.

And then—there she was.

Our little Annie.

She was so small, just 6 pounds, 12 ounces. Her delicate fingers curled instinctively around my thumb, and her warm, milky scent wrapped around me like a comfort I didn't know I'd been longing for. She looked like a baby doll—perfect in every way.

This time, I felt more prepared to be a mother. I wanted to give her everything I hadn't been able to give Mary at that age—all the nurturing and attention I wished I could go back and pour into my first days as a mom.

And Annie made it easy.

When Mary was born, I hadn't felt supported in learning to nurse her. The nurses hadn't emphasized it, and no one had really shown me how. I'd missed out on that bonding experience, and even now, the thought still pricks my heart like a needle.

But with Annie, it was different.

The moment she was born, she latched on as if she'd been waiting for it. Her tiny mouth rooted instinctively, and I felt this wave of relief, gratitude, and connection all at once. She became my most snuggly, lovey baby.

We spent the first four months of her life practically attached to one another.

I know I shouldn't have, but I took naps with her while she nursed. I'd wake to find her still latched, her small body rising and falling in the rhythm of sleep, her little fist resting on my chest. She looked so content and peaceful that I'd just lie there, memorizing her every feature—the wispy lashes against her cheeks, the faint furrow of her brow, her little grunts.

Those months were precious.

I didn't realize how much until later—when Annie grew older and proved to be my most independent child. During many of her teenage years, it felt like she completely shut me out.

And though I'll explain more about that later, part of me still wonders if even then—when she was so little— I already knew I'd one day long for this closeness again.

Chapter 9:

Just Dance

*A*fter Annie was born, I tried to move forward from the trauma of the infidelity scare.

One day, an advertisement arrived in the mail for a dance aerobics class.

As I studied the one-page, double-sided flyer at the kitchen table, I felt a little spark of excitement flicker inside me—a feeling I hadn't felt in a long time.

As a teenager, I'd been a cheerleader and on the dance team. Movement felt familiar to me, like an old friend I hadn't seen in years. I didn't realize how much I'd missed it until that moment.

I decided to give the class a try—and I was hooked from the very first session.

The music pulsed through the studio speakers, and as I followed the choreographed steps to the latest hits, it felt like I was shaking off years of heaviness. I showed up almost every day. Each class became a refuge, a place where I could breathe again.

Before I knew it, I was in great shape.

The owner of the studio often watched me from the back of the room. The classes were growing larger each week, and soon she needed more instructors.

One day, she approached me after class, her face glowing with encouragement.

"Have you ever thought about teaching?" she asked.

That was all it took.

Soon, I was learning routine after routine, practicing until my muscles ached. I signed up for certification, studying every spare moment between work and motherhood. To my delight—and a little bit of disbelief—I passed.

I became an aerobics instructor.

I wore a little headset and the cutest workout clothes. My classes were amazing—not just because of me, but because I loved them, and my students felt that energy.

For the first time in a long time, I felt like I belonged.

I was gaining confidence. I was beginning to let go of the past.

But then came the day that changed everything.

It was a Saturday morning. During the strength portion of the routine, I decided to increase my weights.

As I performed trap pull-ups, I felt a sudden, sharp, and hot pull in my back—like a deep displacement at the base of my spine.

I knew I was hurt, but I pushed through the class with a smile plastered on my face. I didn't want to worry anyone—or admit it to myself.

Afterward, I drove straight to an urgent care clinic. I didn't know what they'd do, but I needed relief.

The nurse practitioner examined me but seemed suspicious, her eyes flicking to me like she was trying to read between the lines of my pain. At the time, her demeanor confused me.

Eventually, she gave me a steroid pack for inflammation and a prescription for tramadol to help with pain.

If I could go back to that day and tell myself not to take the tramadol, I would.

I'd slap it right out of my hand.

That one little pill became the spark that lit my first real opioid addiction.

It started innocently enough.

But later, nothing about my addiction would be innocent.

Everyone got hurt—not just me.

Chapter 10:

Boys Will Be Boys

*L*ife moved forward, and soon we learned baby number three was on the way.

I'll never forget my Leroy's reaction when we found out Anthony was a boy.

He cried.

My husband never cried.

In fact, there were times I wondered if he was emotionally void. He was kind, calm, and steady—but not always emotionally present in the ways I needed. To be fair, I believe he tried. Even now, after our divorce, he's more emotionally present with our children than he ever was with me. It's as if something inside him kept him from fully bonding with another adult.

But with our kids? He was different.

He has always been, and still is, an exceptional father.

Anthony's pregnancy, though, was brutal.

It felt like all I did was cry, sleep, and hurt.

Toward the end, every time I stood up, it felt like my right heel would explode. The pain was unbearable— sharp, radiating up my leg with each step. I cried from morning until night.

By this time, I was working at a nursing home just across the street — but somehow, it still felt too far from home. The girls always played CMT's top hits, probably thinking it would lift my spirits. But any emotion those songs stirred only made me tear up.

The song *God Gave Me You* hit especially hard. It made me grieve the relationship my husband and I had before the shadow of infidelity crept in.

I was reaching a point where I couldn't take much more.

Later, I learned I had ruptured a disc in my back— probably from the injury that started during aerobics. It was some of the worst pain of my life, second only to childbirth itself.

Finally, Anthony arrived.

He was calm from the moment he entered the world, staring up at us as if confused about being outside the womb.

He was beautiful.

But fragile.

When I saw the retractions in his tiny chest as he struggled to breathe, my heart sank.

No matter what anyone says, when something is wrong with your baby, you blame yourself.

We made it through those first terrifying days and finally brought him home.

But unlike with the girls, bonding with Anthony didn't come easily.

The first thing I noticed was that he wouldn't look me in the eye.

He was fussy—crying almost constantly—and rarely smiled.

I tried to rationalize that he didn't smile because he was so young, but when the time came that he should've been smiling back at me, he still didn't.

To make matters worse, he wouldn't latch when I tried to nurse him. After weeks of trying, I developed mastitis and a stiff neck from the effort.

I loved my son deeply.

But I couldn't shake the feeling that he didn't love me back.

The pain of that was unbearable.

And for some reason, six weeks after his birth, I decided to enroll in classes for my BSN.

I was clearly still in a rush, or maybe that's where I found my value—in education.

I told myself it was the right move, that I needed to keep progressing, but the truth was—I wasn't okay.

It didn't last long.

Who could manage college courses under those circumstances?

Soon after starting, I had to withdraw.

That failure sank me into a deep depression.

My mental health was circling the drain, and I knew it.

I didn't know exactly what was wrong—but I knew it was something big.

Chapter 11:

Circling the Drain

*T*his was the beginning of my descent into a major mental health struggle.

For years, I didn't know what was wrong with me, so I did the only thing I knew how to do: I self-medicated.

At first, it was with alcohol and tramadol.

All I knew was that I felt anxious and depressed all the time. A heavy sadness clung to me like a damp blanket I couldn't shake off.

I'd been sad and scared before, but this... this was a different monster.

It felt like something had taken root in my chest, a pulsing, restless energy that kept me awake at night and wore me down by day.

I started having intense mood swings and long periods of insomnia—days on end where it felt like only hours had passed.

Sometimes my thoughts raced so fast I could hardly keep up with them. Other times, they sank like stones into a deep, black water I couldn't see the bottom of.

I also began doing things completely out of character.

I would drink and drive without a second thought, as if some invisible force was daring me to push the limits.

I spent time with shady characters I'd never have associated with before—people whose darkness matched something I felt rising inside me.

I became fixated on strange tasks—organizing or cleaning in obsessive ways—that in the end led to nothing substantial, but ate up hours or even days.

I was scared.

And so were the people around me.

Looking back, I can see now that I was self-medicating what they call hypomania.

I have bipolar disorder, whether I like to admit it or not.

Admitting it—or denying it—doesn't change the fact that the problem exists.

I stumbled through a few years, clinging to my sanity as best I could.

But I never stopped self-medicating.

If it wasn't drugs, it was exercise—running myself to the brink—or limiting my food intake to the point of anorexia.

I went through job after job, struggling with myself and with everyone around me.

It finally came to a head at one of my nursing jobs.

I'd developed a pattern: I'd get my own pain pills, then detox—no matter where I was or what I was doing.

And it wasn't just tramadol anymore.

I'd moved on to heavy hitters like hydrocodone, oxycodone, methadone, and oxycontin.

Obviously, these weren't all prescriptions. I was buying them from people—anyone who would sell.

But no matter how many pills I had—prescribed or bought—they were never enough.

I always wanted more.

Even through all this, I still went to work—high or detoxing.

To me, this was my way of maintaining "normalcy." If I could show up and do my job, then maybe—just maybe—I wasn't as far gone as I feared.

I don't know if the other nurses noticed. Or maybe it didn't matter.

But one night shift, the house supervisor called me into her office.

Her face was tight, unreadable.

"A patient claims you didn't give them their pain medication," she said.

My stomach dropped.

"I know I did," I replied, my voice steady but my pulse pounding in my ears.

By then, I had already passed through the detox portion of my cycle. I wasn't sweating profusely anymore, and I knew I'd test negative for opioids.

So, when they drug tested me, I wasn't worried.

The test came back clean.

But they terminated me anyway.

That was the beginning of the end for me.

It was the moment I lost faith in people—and in the process.

I'd never so much as taken a Band-Aid from work, but none of that mattered now.

My moral compass had been broken for a while, but now it was shattered.

It hadn't happened overnight.

It was a slow fade.

But I was on track for total loss.

And it was happening fast.

Chapter 12:

Triple Trauma

*I*t's no wonder I became the mess I was.

Looking back, I can see it clearly now.

I skipped my childhood and jumped straight into one of the most serious careers there is—nursing.

I'll never forget something a manager once said while coaching staff on leaving their stressors at the door:

"You may be having a rough day, but you are often present for the very worst day of someone else's life."

That stuck with me.

It still does.

One night, I was working a shift at a small rural hospital. In those places, you see everything.

I was in charge of the med/surg unit, which also meant I was part of the code team.

We got a call overhead: *Code Blue for an incoming patient.*

The team gathered in the ER, preparing for whatever was about to roll through the doors.

The ambulance pulled in fast.

They raced inside, a paramedic straddling a teenage boy, performing chest compressions.

He didn't look like a child, but I'd heard it in the nursing report—he was only fifteen.

He was also what we call DOA—dead on arrival.

It sounds harsh, but it was true. He was completely purple.

Then came a sound I'll never forget.

His mother screeched into the ambulance bay, leaping out of her car and screaming bloody murder.

"Nooooo! God, please! Noooooo!"

Her cry pierced through every part of me like shards of glass.

We continued CPR—not for him, but for her.

His father tried to hold her, but she wouldn't accept comfort.

When we finally called the code, I found myself holding the boy's necklace.

I tried to hand it to his mother.

"No! That's my son's necklace!" she wailed, clutching it as if it held his heartbeat.

That night didn't include a single break.

～

Another time, it was a beautiful spring day in April.

I remember driving to work with the windows down, the warm breeze in my hair, feeling lighthearted—like maybe I could handle anything.

That feeling didn't last long.

As soon as I arrived, a code blue was called overhead.

I headed straight for the ER.

The patient was a motorcycle accident victim.

The room was packed with staff, everyone moving with quiet urgency.

I'll never forget his legs.

They were drawn up in a way that told me he had a severe head injury.

The skin on his shins looked... irrelevant. It had peeled up like tissue paper.

He was receiving unit after unit of packed red blood cells. I wondered where the bleed was.

When the paramedic performing compressions needed a break, I took over.

It's exhausting work. Your arms burn, and your heart pounds harder than the patient's failing one.

After a few rounds, I switched to giving respirations for the respiratory therapist.

That's when I saw it.

Instead of hair—or even a skull—I saw the back of his brain.

I think I went into silent shock.

But you can't break down in these moments.

You hold it together, no matter how impossible it feels.

We called the code.

As they pulled the contents of his pockets, I noticed his wedding ring on his hand.

A Taco Bell receipt from fifteen minutes earlier.

Fifteen minutes.

While I was enjoying my sunny drive to work, he was enjoying his last motorcycle ride.

The only difference was that my ride wasn't my final hour of life.

His was.

∾

Then there was the son and his mother.

They were both patients on my unit—she for acute respiratory failure, he for pneumonia.

They were close.

Even from their rooms, they'd talk on the phone constantly, their voices carrying softly through the hall.

She was discharged first.

Later that day, I was in his room doing an assessment when his phone rang.

"Hello? What?! Noooo!!! God, please no!"

He hung up and turned to me, frantic.

"Take me to the ER now!"

As I wheeled him down, he called someone.

"Mom overdosed. She's on her way back to the hospital."

…She didn't make it.

A few days later, I came back from my time off to learn he'd been discharged.

He'd gone home and committed suicide.

This is what nurses face every day.

We're expected to manage this kind of trauma — and then walk into the next room with a smile to hand someone a cup of water they requested six hours ago, as they scold you for having to wait so long.

We preach self-care to our patients, but in this profession, it's frowned upon for nurses to even take a bathroom break—let alone sit down.

It's a culture that eats its own.

No wonder so many nurses become addicts.

We numb the pain—the emotional, psychological, and even physical pain.

Drugs quiet the screams inside.

And sometimes, they're the only thing that does.

Chapter 13:

The Black Sheep's Door

Sometime after all of this, I finally asked my husband the question that had haunted me for years.

"What am I missing? Did you have a relationship with that girl? Did you sleep with her?"

This time, he admitted it.

My gut had been right all along.

I thought hearing the truth would give me peace — at least then I wouldn't feel crazy anymore. But instead, it broke me completely.

We weren't the wholesome couple we pretended to be. Now, we'd dragged our kids into this mess too.

I was furious he chose not to tell me until we'd had another child — although I am so grateful for my son.

I needed to escape. I couldn't take any more pain.

That moment became my breaking point.

I found myself at a family member's house—the so-called black sheep of the family. Everyone knew about their drugs and other illegal activity. I knew if I went there, I'd find an escape.

And I was right.

It wasn't long before I was using meth. A lot of it.

The first time I tried it, I parachuted it—swallowing a half gram wrapped in a piece of paper.

It hit me like a freight train, launching me into another world.

For at least three days straight, I didn't eat, drink, or even use the bathroom.

When I finally came to, I was barefoot and filthy. My urine was almost brown. I stank to high heaven.

And I was gone—mentally, emotionally, spiritually.

I tried to go home.

My husband welcomed me, his eyes full of hope and hurt.

But I couldn't stay. I didn't have it in me to face what I'd just learned—or what I'd just done.

I showered, grabbed some clothes, and left again.

That decision changed the trajectory of my life forever.

Chapter 14:

Levi

*I*t wasn't long before I started hanging around Jackie, a girl I'd met through my drug use.

In the beginning, she seemed fun and inviting—and she always had drugs. Meth. Heroin. Both.

At first, I was more interested in meth. It kept me moving, talking, feeling alive. But doing only that often led to intense paranoia, and I was already an anxious person by nature.

It didn't take long for my old opioid addiction to resurface. Soon I was injecting both—speedballing, as they call it.

Using meth and heroin together took me to another realm entirely. It was a place where nothing felt wrong. Where all my emotional pain disappeared. Where even the shame of my current behavior couldn't touch me.

It was a wonderfully vicious cycle.

∾

Jackie's house was always full of people—some bringing drugs, others buying them.

Then there were those who just stayed for hours or days, floating in and out, hollow-eyed and restless.

I always assumed they were like me: hurt, broken, lost, scared.

People society didn't want—or know how—to deal with.

There was a lot of fear and hopelessness in that house.

And even though I hated the life I was living, I couldn't go back to the one I'd left behind either.

I didn't belong there anymore.

I didn't belong anywhere.

Not long after, a man came to Jackie's house.

He stood quietly in the corner, wearing a hoodie, jeans, and tennis shoes. He looked sheepish somehow—as if he didn't want to be there.

I caught him stealing intense glances at me.

Finally, I asked Jackie, *"What's his name?"*

"Levi," she said.

At first, I didn't even know he used drugs.

Maybe he was just there with the people he came in with. Or maybe he was the dealer.

But there was something about the way he carried himself—quiet and unhurried—that made me want to keep watching him.

It wasn't about being saved. I didn't want or need that.

I wanted him.

His eyes found mine, and it felt like I was the only person there.

There was a gentleness in him I could see from the very beginning, even in a place like this.

Jackie noticed too.

"He's trouble," she warned.

But I couldn't ignore him. No matter how hard I tried, my eyes kept finding his.

The sound of his name lingered in my mind.

Levi.

I didn't know then how deeply that name would carve itself into my heart.

But something in me already knew: This wasn't just another passing face in the chaos.

This was the beginning of something I couldn't stop, even if I wanted to.

Reflection: The Gasp

You hit.

You shoot.

You bang.

The drugs rush into your bloodstream—and you wait.

Gasp.

It takes your breath away.

Your lungs feel like they're on fire—but in a good way.

Suddenly, you feel like you can do it all.

Anything.

Nothing is wrong.

Nothing can touch you.

Nothing hurts—emotionally or physically.

That rush is the reason.

The first rush is always the best.

And you chase it for the entirety of your addiction.

But it's never quite the same again.

It's toxic.

It's never-ending.

And it's destructive...

Until you choose to stop.

Some can.

Others can't.

The ones who can't—often lose their lives.

For some reason... I didn't.

And I thank God for that, every single day.

Chapter 15:

Mine

You need to understand—meth makes a person bold in ways they never were before. It's not just a high; it's a rush that electrifies every nerve. It makes you feel powerful, happy, excited—like possibilities are limitless, like nothing and no one can touch you.

By then, I had already crossed into the valley of no return.

I still remember the first flash of my own blood while injecting myself. I had chosen my vein long before I ever held a needle.

The shot of heroin I prepared that day was brown—looked like dirty water—and in essence, that's exactly what it was. I watched as the liquid swirled in the spoon, the faint chemical smell biting at my nose.

I pulled it up into a diabetic syringe, the plunger moving smooth and sure beneath my thumb. Sliding the needle into the crook of my left arm, I felt the sharp pinch of skin giving way, the slight burn as the metal found its place.

When I pulled back, a stream of dark red blood bloomed into the barrel, curling like smoke in water.

"Ah yes," I thought, as if some part of me had been waiting for this moment. Then I pushed the plunger down, emptying its contents straight into my bloodstream.

In that instant, I understood why people get hopelessly addicted to heroin. Because I was. Right then.

The first time I added meth to the mix, I was addicted to them both—with zero power to stop. That *"blood return"* triggered the same sick sense of satisfaction I'd felt as a nurse seeing a flash of blood while starting an IV. Except this was different. This was deadly.

Not long after, Levi walked back into Jackie's house. I'd just gotten high—speedballing—and felt unstoppable.

The room seemed to hum, my heart pounding fast but steady, my skin warm and alive.

Then I saw him. He looked amazing to me. New. Exciting. The kind of man whose calm draws you in and dares you to stay.

And I wanted him.

I leaned toward Jackie with a smirk, my voice low and certain. *"Watch this. I'm taking him from that girl. He's going to be mine."*

And I did.

I can't recall exactly how it all unfolded after that, but I know this:

I spent the next nine months straight with Levi—day in and day out. To this day, I've never experienced a more intense, all-consuming relationship.

One of our first intimate moments is forever burned into my memory. We were in the shower together, warm water cascading over our bodies, steam curling around us like a veil.

He looked me square in the eyes and said, *"I LOVE YOU!"*

His voice was raw, almost desperate.

Without hesitation, I blurted, *"I LOVE YOU TOO!"*

We were inseparable. Bonnie and Clyde.

Some might say it was just the drugs. And yes, I know the chemicals contributed to our forwardness. But I also know we were truly in love.

From the moment I laid eyes on him, I knew: He was mine. No ifs, ands, or buts.

Chapter 16:

The Russian Supermodel

*A*fter our exchange of I love you, we spent the night together for the first time.

When I woke up the next morning, the room was quiet except for the faint rhythm of Levi's breathing. He lay there on the bed, his dark lashes resting against his cheeks, his chest rising and falling steadily under the thin blanket.

I shifted slightly, careful not to wake him, and let my eyes roam the unfamiliar space. There was a stillness to the air, the kind of quiet that feels almost sacred.

Surprisingly, I wasn't afraid—as you might expect in that situation. Instead, a strange calm settled over me. It felt like the chaos of my life had been momentarily put on pause.

I climbed back into bed gently, the mattress giving a soft squeak beneath my weight. Placing my hand on his chest, I leaned over slightly, my fingers splaying against the warmth of his skin. I didn't want to startle him. I wasn't even sure if he would remember everything from the night before.

"Levi," I whispered softly. *"It's Prudence."*

He stirred, his brows knitting together as his eyes fluttered open. For a moment, he seemed disoriented, blinking hard as if trying to focus.

I didn't realize his eyesight was that bad, I thought.

Then, suddenly, his expression shifted. His lips parted, and his voice came out thick with sleep and surprise. *"Oh my God!"* he blurted, eyes wide now. *"I thought you were an angel! You look like a Russian supermodel."*

A laugh slipped out of me before I could stop it, warm and light. I thought about it for a moment. I was twenty-nine then—young and thin, my freshly washed blonde hair falling in soft waves from sleeping on it damp. My blue eyes and fair skin seemed to glow in the muted morning light filtering through the curtains.

I wore a Victoria's Secret long-sleeve sleep shirt, the fabric soft against my skin, and I still smelled faintly of the lotion and perfume I applied every night after my shower.

Even in the depths of addiction, I hadn't let go of that part of myself—not yet. That would come later, when the drugs had their way with my mind and body.

No wonder he was looking at me like I was one of the seven wonders of the world. A beautiful woman in love with him, clean, quiet, and gently waking him with a soft touch—this wasn't something he saw often.

Now, knowing his story as I do, I understand how disorienting that must have felt for him.

Chapter 17:

Risky Business

Soon, Levi and I were off and running in a world I knew nothing about.

He was wonderfully different—more so than anyone I'd ever known in my life. There was a stillness about him, a quiet strength that seemed unshaken even in the whirlwind of chaos around us.

I'd never experienced such an intense connection with another person, except for my children. But we were also hopelessly addicted—to meth, to heroin, and to each other.

It was a catastrophic difference compared to the woman I'd been before I met him. The strangest part? I didn't care.

Using those two drugs together—injecting them— took me to a place where I still *knew* I was a mother, but I didn't *feel* it. It was as though my heart had gone numb, a protective layer between me and everything that should have mattered most.

The same went for being a wife. I knew my husband was upset, that he wanted me to come home. But I had no desire to return.

I was living in an alternate universe now—one full of magic, intensity, danger, excitement, and risk. Every moment felt sharp and electric, as if I were standing on the edge of a high cliff with the wind whipping through my hair.

Speaking of risk, it wasn't long before we no longer felt welcome—or safe—in Bloomington.

Levi's stepfather had a studio apartment on the corner of 13th and Delaware Street in Indianapolis. He was schizophrenic and rarely stayed there, so the place sat empty most of the time.

As soon as Levi mentioned moving in, a wave of fear rippled through me.

"We can go there to detox and get clean together", he said. The thought of leaving felt heavy, my stomach tightening like a fist.

But strangely, that fear was quickly replaced with relief. Maybe we really could get clean.

Soon, we were packing up and heading toward what we imagined as a fresh start—a new chapter that felt real to us in that moment, even if the foundation was as fragile as glass.

Chapter 18:

Witches & Warlocks

We didn't get clean. It was too difficult to even try. So, back into chaos we spun. Indianapolis was a whole new world to me—a place where strange things happened.

I'll never forget the night Levi took me to a house where I knew no one, but he seemed to know them all. It was nighttime, but the house was buzzing. Music blasted, lights burned in every room, and people drifted in and out like a swarm.

At one point, a man passed through the front room where Levi and I sat. In each fist, he held what looked like massive crystals—like something you'd see a wizard use to cast a spell.

"What is that?" I asked Levi.

"They're shards," he answered.

I sat with it for a moment. Then it hit me. *"That's meth?!"*

It felt fitting. When a person uses meth, their thinking twists. They become hollow inside, spiritually void. I thought of it like some twisted version of a love potion—because the moment you take it, you fall in love with everyone around you.

He smiled—always amused by my innocence. I hated it. The more annoyed I got, the more entertained he seemed. I despised feeling unschooled in that world. I wanted in. I wanted to belong.

But he wouldn't let me. He never said why—he just wouldn't.

After seeing those giant crystal shards, I don't remember much else about that night. I'm sure it was drug-fueled and dangerous. But all I can recall is how stunned I was by the sheer amount of drugs in one place.

And, strangely... it was his ex-girlfriend's house. She was friendly to me, as though someone had cast a spell on her.

Or maybe... we were all under a spell.

Chapter 19:

Father of Lies

We were fully immersed in the world of drugs—using them, selling them, chasing them, and sometimes even loathing them. Our lives became a blur of headlights on highways, cigarette smoke curling in borrowed rooms, and the faint chemical scent that clung to our clothes.

We were always on the move, driving from one place to the next. It was exhausting, but in a strange way, it felt normal—like motion was the only thing keeping us from unraveling completely.

I began noticing something about Levi when he talked to others on the phone.

He lied.

All the time.

It didn't matter who he was talking to—his stories were never fully true. We would be on the way to sell someone drugs, and he would tell them he was on

Highway 67 heading south from Indianapolis when we were really on 46 heading west. Or he'd say we were in a truck when we were in a car—or give the color of a vehicle we weren't even in.

At first, I couldn't make sense of it. Each half-truth scratched at me like a thorn, leaving little cuts I couldn't ignore.

One night, the words burst out before I could stop them. *"You remind me of Satan—the father of lies."*

He didn't respond. Just stared off into the dim light, his face unreadable.

Now I know that in that lifestyle, lies are part of survival. You can't let people know where you are, what you're doing, or who you're with. But at the time, I didn't fully grasp that.

Growing up as a child of God, Levi's constant dishonesty tore at me. I loved him, but I longed for him to be honest—to live in truth.

Still, he had his moments. Almost daily, he'd drawl in his quiet, steady voice: *"Myyyy baby…"* Or sometimes just, *"I love you."*

At first, I soaked up those words like dry earth drinking in rain. But as the drugs pulled us deeper into darkness, they began to sound hollow—echoes in an empty room.

Did he really know what love was? Did I?

One night, in the middle of a drug-fueled, sleep-deprived haze, something inside me snapped. *"You don't know what love is!"* I shouted, my voice cracking with anger and heartbreak.

I grabbed my phone, my fingers trembling as I scrolled through my Bible app. The screen's cold glow lit up my face in the passenger seat of my Impala.

I began reading aloud, my voice shaking but growing stronger with each word:

"Love is patient, love is kind. It does not envy, it does not boast, it is not proud. It does not dishonor others, it is not self-seeking, it is not easily angered, it keeps no record of wrongs. Love does not delight in evil but rejoices with the truth. It always protects, always trusts, always hopes, always perseveres. Love never fails." (1 Corinthians 13:4–8)

Levi stayed silent.

He didn't look at me, but I felt the weight of his stillness. I don't think he'd ever heard anything like that before.

At the time, I believed God had possibly sent me onto a battlefield to meet Levi where he was. Maybe I was there to love him so he could witness my eventual transformation—and long for one of his own.

But first, I had to return to God myself. Because by then, I had fallen far away.

Pain will do that. It'll take you places you never thought you'd go.

Chapter 20:

He Wept

Not long after the night I read Levi the Love manifesto; I told him I was leaving.

"I'm going to rehab," I announced, my voice quiet but resolute.

The truth was, I didn't even know what that meant—or how I'd do it. All I knew was that I couldn't live like this anymore.

The world I'd been moving through—once so intoxicating, so electric—now felt hollow and bitter--it all seemed to press in on me at once.

When I told Levi, something happened that shocked me.

He didn't argue. He didn't rage. Instead, he laid his head in my lap and wept. Not just tears. Full-body, soul-deep weeping.

His shoulders shook violently, his breath coming in ragged gasps as sobs racked his frame. The sound of it filled the small room, raw and unguarded. I had never seen anyone cry like that. Not a man. Not Levi.

"Please don't go," he begged, his voice muffled against my thighs. *"I'll miss you too much."*

But deep down, I knew the truth. He wouldn't have missed me. It was God's presence in me he was afraid to lose.

I don't think Levi would have understood that if I'd said it out loud. Maybe he wouldn't believe it even now.

Still, his weeping pierced me. It made me hesitate. Even though I'd walked into Levi's life in shambles, Jesus was still my Savior. And once you know God, you carry a light no darkness can fully extinguish.

Even in addiction, that shine doesn't disappear. You can be surrounded by darkness, but the light stays within you.

"Levi," I said softly, my fingers brushing his dark hair, *"it's not me you're afraid of losing. It's the Spirit of God."*

But he didn't understand. Or maybe he couldn't. His heart cry persuaded me to stay. I was falling for him—completely.

Chapter 21:

For the Love of Levi

*F*or the love of Levi, I stayed.

Even when I knew I should leave. Even when my soul was crying out for something different.

But at that time, I didn't know how to live without him—or the drugs.

He and I were still trapped in the cycle of using, chasing, and hiding.

It's hard to explain the kind of bond that forms in the midst of that chaos.

When you're shooting up together, coming down together, and surviving close calls together, it creates something that feels unbreakable.

But it's not love—not the kind God intended. It's trauma.

I was aware, on some level, that I'd lost myself. The woman who used to light up rooms was gone. The mother who doted on her children was gone too.

All that remained was a shell.

A woman who'd do anything to stay high—and stay with him.

We drove endless miles in that car, the world outside reduced to a blur of streetlights and shadows.

Every day felt the same: a hunt for drugs, a fight to keep from being dope sick, a desperate attempt to hold our fragile bubble together.

I didn't know then that everything we'd built was already crumbling.

There were moments I looked at Levi and thought:

I love you too much to leave, but I love you too much to stay.

It was a torment I couldn't name.

And so I stayed.

For the love of Levi.

Chapter 22:

Climactic Edge of Desire

The first time I heard "Part II: On the Run," my heart leapt. I had no idea how prophetic that song would become in my life.

"Who wants the perfect love story anyway? Cliché…"

And then…

"What about the bad guy goes good?" Finally— *"I don't care if we're on the run, baby, as long as I'm next to you… I don't care if they give me life, I get all of my life from you…"*

God, that song still hits me like a gut punch.

Even now, when I hear it, I'm taken back to those first moments with Levi—falling wildly, recklessly, irrevocably in love. It was magic. It was electric. It was the kind of love that blotted out the rest of the world.

Later in my life, I'd meet other men and catch myself looking for pieces of Levi in them—hoping, imagining. But no one could ever fill that void.

Levi's eyes were hunter green. He called them hazel, but he didn't see them the way I did. When he looked at me, they softened, moistening as if the very sight of me stirred something deep inside him. His eyes could romance me all on their own.

I once believed Levi was naturally gentle and soft-spoken, but that wasn't true. With others, he was stern—blunt, sharp, impatient. But with me? He melted. He became silly, kind, and playful.

I'd never been with a man so fit—so magnetic. His body satisfied every sense I had. Prison had preserved him, sharpening his edges in all the right ways.

I couldn't get close enough. I needed his skin on mine, his presence wrapped around me. If we weren't together, I was thinking about the next time we would be.

I never thought a man could make a woman climax with penetration alone, but Levi did. He's the only man who ever has. The chemistry between us was a force of nature—like gravity, like magnets snapping together.

There was no stopping it. And I wouldn't have even if I could.

One night stands out more than most. It started out dark—literally and spiritually.

We were staying at the Knights Inn off I-465, and almost immediately, I felt the suffocating sense of a third presence in the room.

They don't tell you that meth rips the veil between the physical and spiritual realms. I saw them—three dark figures crouching in the corner. And I felt them.

I asked Levi if he sensed them. He smiled, calm as ever. *"It's God,"* he said.

No. That was not my God. Maybe it was the god of this world—the god Levi knew.

We got out of there fast.

Later that night, we sat at a Marathon station downtown. I was high out of my mind, rambling— *talking out my neck*, as we called it. I made no sense, slipping in and out of reality, talking to people who weren't even there.

But Levi just smiled at me.

I think… he just loved being with me—no matter what. His love, however twisted by our circumstances, was real. And sometimes, that love grounded me when nothing else could.

Eventually, I came back to myself, and we took off into the night.

I threw on some music—songs that wrapped me in love and romance. John Mayer's "Edge of Desire" started playing just as we pulled off Delaware onto I-70.

The stars were shockingly clear that night, even in the city.

We drove for hours in what felt like a figure-eight—on and off highway ramps, in and out of downtown Indianapolis.

It's rare for a night to start terrifying and end as one of the most romantic of your life. But that night did.

Even though I lost so much to that city, I also gained things I couldn't understand back then. Now, I see it for what it was: we were truly and deeply in love.

I hate that drugs were part of our story. But I've learned that they simply tore down walls— walls of fear, shame, and hiding—so we could expose ourselves to each other in ways we never would have otherwise.

We lived for those moments—alone, naked, tangled in each other's arms.

The drugs stripped away fear. I wasn't ashamed of my flaws anymore. I embraced my sexuality with him. And he embraced him with me.

I'd never been looked at the way Levi looked at me.

When he gazed into me, I fell into him—like we were one. There was no end to me or beginning of him.

The stars may as well have spun around us as we made love on the moon.

Even now, when my mind tiptoes back, I can still feel the cool night air, the weightless floating, the softness of his skin against mine. His touch — firm, gentle — just like his heart. He loved me at my worst.

He saw all of me.

And in his arms, I was finally… free.

Chapter 23:

Cops and Glocks

*I*t was the first time I ever woke up without him there.

The room felt hollow, the quiet so thick it pressed against my ears.

I felt better after sleeping for close to 12 hours, but I was definitely not happy that he was gone.

I looked for my car keys—they were gone too.

Sometimes he took liberties I was certainly not fond of.

As I looked around the apartment to make sure he'd really left, the door swung open.

"You're so lucky right now," I thought to myself, biting back the anger that had been simmering.

I badgered him for a few minutes until I discovered he had drugs.

All was well at that point.

We got high, and soon we were off to the races again.

The buzz in my veins made the world feel sharp, electric.

We drove to Spencer to sell some meth to a girl he knew, which wasn't uncommon.

She him-hawed around about the meeting place, which was also quite common due to paranoia and the fear of being picked up.

They finally settled on a spot—the junction of highways 67 and 231.

As we sat there, I pulled down the visor and started doing my makeup.

Habits played low on the stereo.

"This song's quite fitting," I thought, smudging liner along my lashes.

I glanced over at Levi as he divided up 10 or more grams of meth and about 3 grams of heroin into tiny baggies.

"God, that's a lot of dope," I thought, my stomach tightening even as I felt the high humming through me.

Just as the thought crossed my mind, headlights appeared, cutting across the lot.

Relief flooded me—I thought we were about to get this over with.

I was ready to get on with the magical evening I was sure we'd have that night.

Until—

Whoosh, whoosh, WHOOSH!

A car, then a cruiser, and finally an SUV, all spewed into the parking lot with lights flashing like a hundred angry hornets.

"DON'T MOVE! PUT YOUR HANDS BEHIND YOUR FUCKING HEAD NOW!"

They dragged Levi from the car and crashed him into the gravel.

I peered through the driver's side window and into the face of a Glock.

The metal gleamed under the flashing blue lights.

I admit, it was… exciting in a way I couldn't explain.

I looked at the cruiser, its lettering glowing in the strobes: **Bloomington Meth Task Force.**

My heart thudded in my ears.

Quickly, they separated us into different cars.

I sat stiffly with an officer who looked familiar.

A state trooper sat beside me—the same one who had stopped us months earlier on our way to Indy, back when I'd first met Levi.

That officer had snidely asked me what I was doing with Levi then.

"Where's your husband and family?" he asked. Just then I realized…

It was my husband's birthday. It was October 21, 2014. I was angry that he thought I was just out being a menace to society. *What about the menace to my marriage?* I thought heavily.

Now I was putting it together—they'd been watching us all along.

I'd never had so much as a traffic ticket before this, much less gone to jail.

I was completely out of my element.

As far as I knew, I was headed to jail that night.

Somehow, though, within an hour, I was back in my car and headed to Indy—to the apartment Levi and I had shared. However, Levi went to jail. It made me sick.

He was gone again. Earlier, I knew he'd come back. This time, I had no idea if or when that would happen.

There was a lot of his absence that day.

They took him, and it would be almost a month before I saw him again.

I was in this addiction life deep now.

And I was in it alone.

As I left the scene that night, I had no idea how to get back to the apartment.

I didn't care, I left as fast as I could—as if the cops would change their minds and start chasing me.

Somehow, I managed to recall enough landmarks to get back to the apartment. When I got back, it felt like everything had just stopped. Dead in the tracks. *What do I do now?* I thought.

Chapter 24:

The Accident

*E*xactly ten days later, I wrecked my car.

I'd been on a meth-fueled binge and decided it would be a good idea to drive back to Bloomington to see if I could find more.

The problem was, I'd also taken a Valium because I was feeling anxious.

The next thing I remember was the violent jolt of being thrown forward into my steering wheel.

The sound of screeching metal. The sharp, acrid scent of burned rubber. A dull ringing in my ears.

I'd slammed into a telephone pole.

I reached for my chest, convinced it was caved in— but I could breathe just fine. I wiggled my fingers, my toes. Somehow, everything worked. Somehow, I was unscathed. *"Should I run and say someone stole my car?"* I thought, my mind racing in panic.

But I knew better.

Thank God I had enough sense to at least stay and face my consequences.

In the distance, I noticed people crouched over, their figures blurred by the distance.

I fumbled for a lighter, my hands trembling as I tried to light a cigarette.

The flame flickered once—then a voice barked:

"PUT IT DOWN!"

Before I knew it, the police had arrived, their blue and red lights strobing across the scene like jagged lightning.

"Did you know you hit that man?!" the officer shouted.

"I hit someone?" I asked, my stomach turning.

I had.

He was lying about fifty feet away from the accident scene, clinging to life. I felt... nothing. No panic. No horror. Just numbness.

The strangest thing—even to me—was that I'd been an ortho/neuro nurse for years before this. I had cared for exactly these kinds of patients.

Yet here I was, standing there emotionless. I even wanted to care... but I didn't.

I sat in the back of a cruiser for what felt like hours, dozing in and out of consciousness while they sized up the scene.

Through the window, I saw flashes—people taking pictures of me as I sat there. I didn't care.

I knew what this amounted to: trouble—and the probable loss of my freedom.

At the hospital for toxicology tests, the officer stayed with me.

He wasn't angry. His face was calm, almost... sad.

I could see empathy in his eyes, and for a moment, it caught me off guard.

As we waited for a nurse, a woman caught my eye through a tinted glass window.

Her face was slightly familiar, but I couldn't quite place her. We exchanged glances a few times before she approached my bedside.

"It's Wendy," she hissed, her voice sharp.

It hit me like a slap. Wendy. The woman who had been my maid of honor at my wedding.

"Where's Mary?!" she demanded, her tone thick with disgust. "You're just a shadow of who you used to be."

Her words sliced deep.

She processed the testing and paperwork quickly.

"Do you just want to go?" she asked flatly.

Of course I did.

I grabbed my things as fast as I could and left the hospital—now on foot.

The city felt enormous and foreign.

The November wind cut through my thin clothes, and I shivered.

It was cold. The city was too big; it felt like I was being swallowed by a place I didn't even know how to navigate. I had always left the directions up to Levi. And I was scared.

I was without a car and alone in a city I knew nothing about.

Bridge the Gap

Levi spent a month in jail. Thirty days — I was alone.

And truthfully, I don't remember much from that period of time.

I felt lost. But something happened: I learned how to survive. On my own.

It was the first time in my life that it was just me. I stayed high all the time.

And when I did sleep, I'd dream he was beside me — like nothing had changed. Then I'd wake up to the harsh truth: He was locked away, and I didn't know if I'd ever see or hear from him again.

But eventually, he was released. He called the moment he got back to the VOA.

Soon after, he came racing to the apartment to see me. When he got there, I hugged him... but something felt off. He felt like a stranger.

Still, we fell right back into spending all our time together.

Chapter 25:

The Dig

*S*till, deep down, I knew there was something real and good—healthy, even—about what Levi and I shared.

I can't count how many times I sat there, needle in hand, desperately searching for a vein I could hit. My arms were shot—bruised, track-marked, the veins collapsed or hidden deep below the surface. Sweat beaded on my forehead as I jabbed again and again—wrist, hand, anywhere I could think of—trying to get the rush my body craved.

Sometimes I'd sit like that for what felt like hours. Jab. Miss. Pull out. Jab again.

And Levi would sit there with me, silent at first, his green eyes glassy with tears.

Finally, he couldn't hold it back anymore. *"This isn't the life you were meant for,"* he whispered, his voice cracking. *"Please… please stop. Let's both get clean. Let's do this right."*

But I wasn't ready to hear it. *"Just stop it, Levi,"* I snapped. *"I'm not quitting. So just drop it."*

What I didn't understand then was why he got so emotional. Why all the tears? Why the desperate pleading?

This is who we are, I told myself. What else would we even be doing if it wasn't this?

But now, looking back, I see what he was mourning.

He was grieving health. Grieving love. Grieving the possibility of true happiness—the kind neither of us believed we deserved, but deep down he still hoped for.

Levi knew this life inside and out. He'd been here before. He knew where it ended, and he was terrified of watching me slide into the same pit he'd spent years trying to claw his way out of.

This drug life was still new to me. I'd stumbled through pills and alcohol before, but nothing as consuming, as vicious as this.

I think he saw a version of me—a brighter, softer version—that I'd long ago surrendered to the world's chaos. He wanted that woman back.

But I didn't know if I could find her again. How could I offer her to someone who had already watched me destroy my body, my mind, my life? And furthermore, why would he even want someone like that?

Chapter 26:

Thanks for Not Giving

*B*y then, I was so far gone that even basic human survival didn't matter. The hunger that clawed at my stomach was faint and distant, like an echo I could barely hear.

It was Thanksgiving.

I sat in Levi's dad's apartment, cold and alone. The electricity had been shut off weeks earlier after the bill went unpaid, and now the November air inside felt almost as biting as it did outside.

From the hallway came the smells of life I no longer knew: roasted turkey, sweet potatoes thick with cinnamon, bread baking in warm ovens. The scents drifted under the door and into my hollow little world, taunting me.

Somewhere above me, laughter rang out, followed by muffled voices and clinking dishes.

I sat still, staring at nothing. My stomach twisted, cramping from days without food.

Out of sheer desperation, I picked up the phone and called my aunt.

When she answered, her voice carried that familiar warmth—the sound of home I'd long since burned to the ground.

"Hey – it's Prudence," I said softly. *"Do you think you could... maybe send me a pizza?"*

There was a pause—angst—filled the brief silence. Then, gently: *"No, Prudence. But I can come pick you up tomorrow when we go Black Friday shopping—and take you to rehab."*

Her words hit like a sucker punch.

It wasn't anger in her voice. It wasn't even a disappointment. It was love—the hard, unyielding kind that stops handing out lifelines because they've seen what you do with the resources you're provided with – self-destruction.

I understood. God, I understood.

But the ache in my chest spread like fire.

I hung up the phone and sat in silence, staring at the faint light coming through the window. My stomach knotted harder.

If I could just find *anything* to eat—even a corn cob, I thought, staring blankly at the trash can outside. Just something to fill me up for a while.

That's where I was.

If I couldn't love myself enough to eat...

If I couldn't stop stabbing poison into my veins...

How could I ever love anyone else properly?

Later that night, Levi called.

"Come see me," he said. *"I've got something for you to eat."*

When I showed up, he was waiting, his green eyes still red-rimmed but softer now. He held out a white boxed meal, the kind they handed out at the VOA—and pushed it gently toward me.

"They gave me a Thanksgiving meal for you," he said quietly.

I stared down at it. Turkey, mashed potatoes, and a dinner roll. Steam curled faintly from the plastic lid.

"You're not going to eat?" I asked.

"I already did," he answered.

In that moment, I couldn't look at him.

This man—wrecked and homeless, as hollowed out by addiction as I was—still found it in himself to give. Even in the gutter. Even with nothing. Levi still gave.

I later discovered that he never ate that night; it was the meal he had given me.

The days that followed were some of the coldest, loneliest, and scariest of my life. This was when I officially became homeless.

The key to the apartment Levi and I had been staying in had disappeared, and the building was locked tight.

Sometimes I could sneak in when others felt inclined to open the door for me, but people knew I didn't belong there.

I had never felt more displaced in my life.

Chapter 27:

Sugar Daddy

*S*oon, I was on dark websites looking for *sugar daddies.*

And boy, did I find them.

At this point, I'd connected with an older, wealthy man who agreed to pay for an apartment for me at The Pointe in Bloomington.

He still worked—an IT executive of some kind, I think. He was also married.

This is the type of situation drugs put you in.

If you want to test a man's character, expose him to a drug-addicted woman and see how he treats her.

I was treated very poorly by many men—unexpectedly so.

Levi, however, never treated me with contempt or disrespect. He may have been deep in that same lifestyle, but as much as he was able, he protected me, stood by me, and loved me no matter what condition I was in.

He never rejected me for anything I did—and I did a lot of bad things.

In addition to the executive, there was a wealthy old farmer who let me sleep in a spare bedroom when I needed it.

He loaned me his Expedition, took me to Florida, and gave me money—always at a cost.

My dignity. My self-respect. My value as a human being.

During this time, I became utterly disgusted with men in general.

Because of the position I was in, I became the subject of their carnal desires.

There were a few times when I was confused to discover that the men only wanted to cuddle or talk, but that disgusted me, too.

Regardless, I needed a way to survive, and they knew it. I would challenge any man reading this: If you ever encounter a woman in a situation like mine, will you help her or take advantage of her?

If you don't know the answer, I implore you to examine that part of yourself. Cleanse it. Correct it.

People—especially women—need men to protect, respect, and help us when we're down… not kick us.

Eventually, Levi got out of jail and returned to the VOA in Indianapolis.

Times were tumultuous, but we made the best of it.

One thing never changed—Levi's gentleness.

We spent a few more months together, but over time, things began to unravel.

The car accident had resulted in a felony warrant for my arrest. I was always running from it.

Somehow, I'd kept my felony charges in Bloomington (the nursing/drug-related ones) under control. I never missed a court hearing and complied with everything I'd agreed to.

I thank God for that every day, because I believe that's what ultimately allowed me to save my career, though it was still an uphill battle.

Chapter 28:

Sex Sells

I stayed in my apartment at The Pointe, and Levi remained at the VOA. I had no choice but to earn money from home, and everyone knows—sex sells.

So, I became Angel Blue Eyes.

Yes, I did webcam work.

In my mind, it was better than the alternative. *At least they can't touch me,* I thought. *At least I can choose when I perform.*

Don't get me wrong—it was degrading.

But it felt like the lesser of two evils.

If you know anything about drugs, you know the kinds of behavior and scenarios that come along with them.

During this time, I had to drive back and forth between Bloomington and Indianapolis to see Levi. Levi being in the VOA was a hindrance to our relationship, but not as much as his being locked up.

He would find ways to get out for a few hours so we could see each other.

I remember one drive up from Bloomington to see him. Music poured through my Bluetooth speaker as always.

"When your legs don't work like they used to before, and I can't sweep you off of your feet..." Ed Sheeran's voice filled the car, soft and aching.

As much as I loved Levi, I also knew we'd started in an unhealthy place—and had ended up in a much worse one.

Still, my heart clung to this idea of a healthy relationship between us.

Our love felt real. It *was* real.

It was hard to reconcile that thought with all the ugliness that had happened between us, but I knew something in him wanted more for us.

He often talked about getting clean together and becoming a *power couple*.

I thought he sounded ridiculous.

"That will never happen," I told myself—or maybe even said out loud to him.

~

One morning, we spent together, and we fell asleep at his dad's apartment. Levi had been gone from the VOA too long. Suddenly, Levi's probation officer burst through the door while we were asleep. He took Levi away—thankfully just back to the VOA. But it was devastating, and how many times would it just be the VOA until it was prison again? I couldn't bear the thought.

I went back to my apartment at The Pointe, alone.

Soon after, I had my first hearing in Bloomington about my drug charges. I was detained for my charges in Indy. It was my very first arrest.

I spent a week or so in jail, and to my surprise, Levi bonded me out. He'd also run from the VOA. Now, he also had a warrant.

When I first got out, I felt relief. But the truth is, after that, we spiraled out of control even faster.

I lost my apartment in Bloomington after the manager at The Pointe discovered my arrest. I couldn't even do webcam work anymore.

I was lost.

So, Levi and I hid out for as long as we could. I still had the Expedition, which allowed us to get around a bit, but it was too risky to move much. We both knew our time was running out.

We'd drive back to Indy every so often.

Levi and I stayed together as much as we could, but we became wanderers, so at times we weren't able to. That created a rift in our relationship. We were beginning to become estranged from one another.

Chapter 29:

Houdini

*I*t was one of the most degrading times in my life.

One night, we slept in an abandoned house—so that we could be together.

It was a house his friend had grown up in, so Levi knew it well. I didn't care—I was just happy there was a bed.

But the relief didn't last long.

The next morning, the cops busted through the door.

I had already violated house arrest because I was homeless, so I had a warrant. Levi did too at that point, but he was like Houdini with the cops.

He gave them a fake name, and when I agreed that it was his name, they let him go.

I thought he'd bond me out again, like before.

But this time… he never came.

My heart was broken. And I was furious.

I spent about three weeks in jail before I remembered a guy I thought might bail me out if I led him to believe I was interested in him.

I was right. Soon, I was out again.

Within 24 hours, I violated house arrest—again—because I had nowhere to go.

I didn't care anymore.

I just wanted to get out of jail and find Levi.

When I finally found him, I don't even remember the time we spent together. Drugs will do that to your memory.

Everything became a blur.

We started spending more and more time apart, and I started staying at a drug house. Levi wasn't welcome there. I was because I was a woman.

And then, I reached a breaking point.

I knew I couldn't keep living like this.

I wanted to find and tell Levi, spend one more beautiful night with him, and then throw up the white flag.

I called a childhood friend and told her what I was planning. I reasoned that if I got her involved, I'd actually go through with it.

My plan was to turn myself in and reclaim my life.

She gave me a ride to Indy.

But first, I had to see Levi.

I'd already gotten rid of everything, so I'd have no excuses, no resources to back out.

My husband had told me that if I turned myself in that day, he'd help me. He'd put money on my books and support me through rehab.

That gave me just enough courage to move forward.

I was so grateful my friend let me call Levi from her phone. He agreed to meet us.

Eventually, we ended up alone.

That's what I wanted. One last night with him before I turned myself in.

We drove around for a while, but soon I felt the pull again.

I asked him to stop at a gas station so I could use the bathroom.

I went inside the Marathon station on the corner of 38th and Lafayette.

I had no idea I was about to step into one of the most heartbreaking moments of my life.

I thought I was ready. I thought I had it all planned — one last night with Levi, then I'd finally surrender and get help. But the universe had other plans. I still had more heartbreak to endure. More to lose. The truth is, I wasn't done yet — not with the chaos, not with him, and definitely not with the pain. I didn't know it, but I was about to face the moment that would finally break me open.

Chapter 30:

Third Time's a Charm

I guess the ride was over.

Levi was gone.

He'd driven off into the sunset with someone else— or at least, that's how it felt.

We'd been derailing for a while. I knew I wanted to change, but I also wanted one more night with my beau.

Levi had been my knight in shining armor in the middle of my hell on earth.

I found him against some pretty hefty odds.

We'd been spending more and more time apart, and I hated it.

I wanted to be with him. Always.

I wanted our love to conquer a multitude of sins. It had before.

Levi had a way of showing up in the most unlikely circumstances.

No matter how badly I messed up, just when it seemed hopeless, he'd appear.

But not this time.

He left me there.

It was something I never thought I'd experience in a million years.

I'd gone into the gas station bathroom to bang, and as usual, it took longer than it should have.

When I came out, I was stunned.

So stunned, in fact, that I waited, sure he'd pull back around at any moment.

I looked and looked... but nothing.

He was gone.

And my heart broke into pieces.

As I looked up at the sky, I noticed for the first time in months how beautiful the sunset was.

And then I heard it—God's voice. *"It's time. It's over."*

I had wanted to spend one last night with Levi before turning myself in on a warrant.

But unbeknownst to me, I had already seen the last of him in the free world.

For the next ten years.

I looked ahead and saw a police officer filling his cruiser with gas.

Again, God spoke: *"Do you want a ride?"*

"No!" I screamed inside.

I've never wanted someone to come back so badly, but Levi didn't.

I should've taken the ride, but I told myself, *"I want to be the one to turn myself in."*

So, I spent the next 12 hours fighting my way downtown to the city-county building, sadder than I'd ever been in my life.

When I got there, I sat on the steps for hours, thinking.

And then… I did it.

I surrendered my freedom.

For the third—and final—time, I walked into the processing center at Marion County.

I hated every step.

My heart ached more with every passing minute as I was moved from one holding cell to the next.

As I took my final steps to be cleared by medical staff—people who had once been my peers—I heard a familiar voice call out:

"Prudence! I love you!"

My heart skipped a beat.

It was him.

Levi.

"I love you too!" I mouthed back as I passed his holding cell. I was in shock.

He was crammed into a small space with at least twenty other men, but somehow, he was standing where I could see him… hear him… feel him.

God gave me the goodbye I needed.

But it wasn't really goodbye.

It was *until we meet again.*

For the next ten years, I couldn't stop thinking about it.

How was all of this even possible?

I'd experienced some of the most wonderful and terrible times of my life—all wrapped into one chapter.

I had been more confused and yet clearer than I'd ever been before.

Looking back, I realize now—that's what kept the fire burning for a decade.

Later, I learned Levi wasn't even supposed to be in the processing center.

His charges were federal, and someone had made an error.

But I'm glad they did.

It felt like fate. And I will be forever grateful for that impossible, one-in-a-million chance encounter.

Chapter 31:

Don't You Forget About Me

*D*on't touch that TV!" I growled.

I'd been watching *Love & Hip Hop* for days.

Being in jail was bad enough—wondering if I'd ever see Levi again made it worse.

But that Saturday morning, something unexpected happened.

The *Breakfast Club* came on TV.

It pulled me back to a more normal place and time in my life, and I needed that.

Surprisingly, the typically loud, mouthy, rude girls on the block left the TV alone. They didn't argue, didn't fuss. They just let me watch.

Quietly.

As I sat there staring at the screen, all I could think about was Levi—how he was gone and out of my life.

Forever.

Or so it seemed.

The sadness was overwhelming, but it gave me space to refocus.

I made a decision.

"I'm getting my life together," I told myself.

That was it.

I was done with the drugs.

I would call my husband and tell him I wanted to go to rehab. I needed his help to get into a program.

I knew he'd be elated to hear it.

We could try to make things work.

We all deserved that—especially the kids.

They needed their parents.

And I needed me.

The nurse in me.

The one with morals, truth, and courage pouring out of her being.

I knew she was still in there somewhere.

As the movie rolled into its final scene, *Don't You (Forget About Me)* started playing.

Tears welled up in my eyes.

All I could think about was Levi and me—what we'd been through, where we were headed, and whether we'd ever see each other again.

One thing was certain:

I would never forget about him.

But deep down, I wondered— *Would he forget about me?*

Part 2:

Ascension

Chapter 32:

Rehab

*F*inally, the day came. On August 1, 2015, I got out of jail. My husband bonded me out and drove me straight to rehab. We wound through the country roads, his truck's broken air conditioning blasting nothing but hot air. The windows were down, but it didn't help much—only stirred the thick humidity and road dust around my face. I wasn't used to moving air—much less a long car ride. The semis spewed fumes that made me sick to my stomach. The landscape blurred by in waves of summer green, but all I could think was: This is going to be an uphill battle. Nothing about it would be easy.

When we arrived, I stared at the facility in disbelief. It sat right on the main drag of town, wedged in like part of a strip mall. No trees. No long driveway. Just a squat, brick building at the end of the row of offices and shops. I hated it already.

Everything seemed to take forever once I got there— especially finding work. I needed a social security card, but my wallet had been stolen during my using days. Every step forward was met with a roadblock. Nothing went right. I was exhausted and grouchy all the time, snapping at people for no reason.

To pass the days, I threw myself into anything I could—reading, cleaning (I became the facility's chore coordinator), and even jewelry making. I loved that hobby. The beads in my fingers gave me something to do, something to build. Still, I felt shackled to my past. I wore a big, black, ugly ankle monitor—and believe me, I wanted to cut it off and run. I almost did once. My freedom felt like it was always just out of reach.

Then, thank God, I finally got a job at the local turkey factory.

I'll never forget my first day. They put me on a line, staring at trays of turkey rolling past under fluorescent lights, making sure nothing hung off the sides. The smell was metallic and cold—like wet meat and sanitizer. My hands froze. My feet ached. The noise of conveyor belts and shouting supervisors echoed around the freezing plant. What have I done to my life? I thought.

My mind drifted constantly—to Levi, to the drugs. I wanted to escape this sad, frozen version of my life. I felt like I was fading.

I think it was my second day when I noticed a girl with a clipboard and a giant thermometer. She stabbed it into a vat of turkey meat, jotted down the temperature, and moved on. She was busy—always on the go, her breath clouding in the air like fog.

God, whatever she's doing... please, let me do that! I prayed.

The very next day, the supervisor approached me. I could see her breath in the cold air.

"Hey, you're a nurse, right?"

"Yes," I answered, my heart skipping.

"So... you're good at documentation?"

I said again.

"I've got a position for you. You'll be taking over for Carrie," she said.

Just then, the girl with the thermometer walked up.

Oh my God! Thank You! I thought. I could hardly believe it—God had answered my prayer overnight. I wouldn't have to stand there, mindlessly losing my mind. I wouldn't have to go numb to survive a shift. *Maybe… maybe I can actually do this*, I thought.

It wasn't easy, but it became possible. The chance to move around changed everything. From that day forward, I worked every shift I could, walking constantly. I loved it. The rhythm, the structure, the sense of purpose—it was medicine.

Chapter 33:

Angel of Light

A few months later, my ankle monitor came off. I started getting passes and going out again. I felt... human. The feeling of walking without that plastic weight digging into my skin was surreal. I'd forgotten what it meant to feel light.

I spent a total of nine months in that program because I needed to, and it changed me—for the better. Slowly, day by day, the fog began to lift.

Toward the end, a young man at the factory took a shine to me. He flirted constantly. And honestly... he was cute: blonde hair, blue eyes, a strong jawline with a dimple in his chin. He had a perfect smile and straight teeth—a real country boy in leather boots, sun-kissed from farm work. He worked on his grandfather's farm when he wasn't at the factory, and he was in great shape—the kind of guy who could lift fifty-pound feed bags without breaking a sweat.

We sat together at meals. I passed his department several times a day, never once without getting a mischievous wink. He asked me to go horseback riding once—I wanted to go but said no.

He was a good distraction... but I knew I had to let him go, too.

So, I came up with a foolproof plan— I carried my Bible with me. Everywhere.

And something incredible happened. I started reading it constantly.

Over three years, I read it from cover to cover—in chronological order. I underlined passages, wrote notes in the margins, cried into the pages. I even did word studies. The Bible is deep.

I took my time, letting it come alive for me. I could see the scenes in my mind—Moses parting the sea, David facing Goliath, Jesus breaking bread. More importantly, I could apply its truth to my own life.

It changed me. Forever.

Even now, I'm infused with the Word of God. Anytime a challenge comes my way, scripture rises up in me like a well.

As for that young man—my plan worked. The Bible literally became my shield.

He backed off, just as I'd hoped.

He had come as an angel of light. But I knew better.

Satan doesn't come ugly—he comes as everything you ever wanted, wrapped up with ease on a silver platter. But the fall is fast. And harsh.

I saw it for what it was—a distraction.

And I was grateful. I was starting to see life clearly again. I was healing.

I graduated from the program in April of 2016. I rejoined my family. I started living with integrity again.

My husband Leroy had his wife back. And my kids… They had their mother.

Chapter 34:

Recovery

I was living a recovered life. I spent another five years with my husband Leroy and our three kids. I mentored women in the same program I had graduated from. For three years, I poured over the Bible in detail, its pages worn and marked with ink and tears. God spoke to me deeply through those verses—sometimes in whispers, sometimes in thunder. This was my time of restoration. He was healing my mind.

But even in this season, I still kept track of Levi. He was back in prison, and I missed him—maybe as much as I did the day he left me at that gas station. The ache was sharp, buried beneath layers of structure and sobriety. I knew in my heart: if given the chance, I would have run off with him and thrown my life back to the wolves. I wasn't strong enough yet.

I filed a restraining order against him because the time came for him to get out of prison—I didn't do that because I hated him, but because I needed a wall between me and the temptation. Love can be dangerous when you're not healed.

At the same time, I fought to rebuild my nursing career. I was on probation with my license. Enrolled in ISNAP. Regular probation, too. The weight of it all felt crushing—meetings, reports, screenings, and daily hoops to jump through. It was grueling.

I continued working in the turkey factory during rehab and excelled even there. I had the chance to manage a department, but deep down, I knew nursing was my calling. God confirmed it when the woman who was to interview me for a management position asked, *"Are you sure you wouldn't consider going back to nursing?"*

That was all I needed to hear. I didn't need another sign.

On June 1, 2016, I had been exactly one year clean and sober. That same day, I stood before the nursing board, praying every step up to the front: Please, God. Give me another chance.

The room was packed, but case by case it cleared. I was the last to be called. It was just me and the board. I approached with humility and confidence, laying out the ugly truth: homelessness, needles, drugs... and now, recovery.

They were stunned, but somehow, they still said yes.

At that moment, I felt a piece of Prudence click back into place. I was whole again.

My mind flashed to one of my darkest nights in addiction—I'd been sick with an infection, alone and terrified, yet I managed to walk to the ER in the dead of winter. I was shivering from fever and withdrawal. I longed for a nurse to come and love on me, to say, *"This is the way out. Let me show you."*

But no one came.

Instead, a nurse approached with an IV kit, aiming for a vein I'd long since destroyed. *"Please don't use that one,"* I said softly. She kept going anyway. When I jerked my arm away, she jumped back and glared at me like I was an insect.

I waited until she walked off to cry. And in that moment, I prayed: God, if You deliver me from this, I'll be the nurse I needed tonight.

And He did.

Later, as a nurse, I noticed how often staff didn't know how to treat addicted patients. They made jokes. They brushed them off. And I couldn't tolerate it.

I became a missionary in a hospital for people struggling with addiction.

Many patients I cared for in the hospital later crossed my path again as I mentored at the recovery center. I saw both ends of their stories—and they saw mine.

Sometimes, the only way to fix what's wrong in the world is to become the solution yourself.

God has blessed me abundantly. *"Now to him who is able to do immeasurably more than all we ask or imagine, according to his power that is at work within us..."* —Ephesians 3:20

Chapter 35:

I'm Back

On August 1, 2016, I officially began my nursing career again. It was just a small nursing home, but I couldn't have been happier to don my scrubs that morning; they were hot pink. The floors smelled of disinfectant. The halls echoed with old TVs and oxygen machines. The pace was steady, the faces familiar. I was being restored day by day.

I was living with complete gratitude. I had never been prouder to put on a pair of scrubs in my life. I wore them like armor. I cared for those patients as if they were my own family.

During this time, my assistant pastor was a missionary who traveled all over the world. I had always felt the tug to travel and minister, too. One day, the opportunity arose: I was invited to Haiti to help hold a medical clinic.

I raised funds by making jewelry—beads between my fingers again, but this time with purpose. I gathered free medical supplies to bring along, tucking ointments and gauze into plastic bins like treasure.

The flight to Haiti was beautiful. I peered out the window and down at the blue-green water. The sand had swirled into a circular shape—white sand. I felt so blessed. I don't know who else would be able to get a passport with pending felonies to go out of the country, but somehow, I did.

Haiti felt foreign and familiar all at once—odd, yet such a blessing. I'd never seen a more beautiful place, but I had also never witnessed such destruction. Port-au-Prince was still in shambles from the 2010 earthquakes. The buildings stood broken and unrepaired, like skeletons of what had been. Trash covered the streets. There was no sanitation, and animals wandered freely through the water supply. People danced and practiced voodoo on street corners under the blazing sun.

We were told the government was corrupt and dangerous. As Americans, we were seen as incredibly wealthy — and to many in other countries, we are. Because of the risk of kidnapping, we traveled in the back of a truck, locked inside a metal cage. And I loved it. I loved risking it all for God.

It took hours to reach our destination, and as we bumped along the dusty roads, I prayed silently: Lord, if it's Your will, let me see the ocean. I'm a sucker for a beautiful beach view.

When we arrived, we found ourselves in a small village still reeling from the devastation of a recent hurricane. Makeshift homes leaned against one another, patched together with tarps and sheets of tin. Barefoot children ran through the dust, their radiant white smiles shining in stark contrast to their surroundings. Despite their hardship, their joy was palpable. They welcomed us with open arms, and it was clear they were genuinely glad we had come.

It was difficult to describe the feeling. I knew I was blessed, but here I understood just how wealthy we are in America—and not just because of money.

The very moment we stepped onto the village street, a woman approached me with her baby. She gently showed me a small rash on the child's bottom. The translator said, *"She asks what this is and if there's a cure. She can't heal it."*

The desperation in her eyes pierced me.

It was just diaper rash. I went back to my supply bag, poured out some zinc cream, and gave her simple instructions on how to use it.

Two days later, she came to the clinic again. The rash had healed. *"Merci,"* she said, tears in her eyes.

Such a small act, but it brought her such joy.

True to God's nature, the village was right on the ocean. The water stretched out like glass with mountains in the background. The view was breathtaking. The climate was tropical, and the salt air felt like freedom.

I was in heaven—serving God in paradise.

The villagers treated us like royalty. Guards watched over us as we slept. They fed us fresh seafood every day—steamed lobster, pumpkin soup, coconut milk, straight from the coconut shell—and escorted us everywhere we went.

On our last day, the bishop drove us a few miles down the road. I wasn't sure what he had planned, but I was content to follow.

We pulled up and over a hill—and suddenly the view exploded into the most tropical, white-sand beach

I had ever seen. Palm trees lined the cove. Dried coconut shells littered the sand.

The sun shone brightly overhead and warmed my skin like a kiss. The water was clear; there was an aqua tint to it, but it was clear.

I still have one I brought home.

God had heard my prayer and answered it far beyond my wildest imagination.

Soon after this trip, I was given a fantastic opportunity, and I took it.

Chapter 36:

Full Circle

The day had come—I got the job! I was back, working in a hospital setting. It was a dream come true. I was on a busy med/surg unit, doing what I loved.

Just two short years before, I had walked through the front entrance of that beautiful hospital with a heart that felt cracked open. I looked around, taking in how clean and serene everything was. The floors gleamed under soft, diffused lighting. Professionals moved with quiet confidence through the corridors. I remember watching a man in a white coat cross a balcony on the second floor, his stethoscope draped around his neck like a badge of honor.

"God, I want to work alongside professionals like that again," I prayed—almost in passing.

And then it happened. God answered my prayer. Again.

A few months into working on that very unit, I was overjoyed—not just to be there, but because I was on a mission. I had become the nurse I once needed. I sought out every addicted patient I could find. I prayed with them, sat on the edge of their beds, held their hands, and shared my story. I coached other nurses and doctors on how to care for them with compassion. I had become the advocate I had promised God I would be.

I did that work for nearly two years.

I even pitched the idea to create a team dedicated to that mission. Eventually, the hospital built a program around it. I wasn't included in it—but I made peace with that. Because it was never really about me, it was about making sure people battling addiction got the help, care, and love they deserved.

Over time, I got to know many of the doctors. One stood out—Dr. Stewart, the hospital's cardiologist. He was especially kind. Our floor had telemetry monitors so we could manage cardiac patients, and one day, something incredible happened.

A patient's monitor showed a strange tachycardic rhythm. I stood there, watching the erratic waves pulse across the screen. Then Dr. Stewart came around the corner and stopped beside me, his eyes scanning the same rhythm.

And in that moment—it hit me.

He was the same professional I had seen on that balcony years before, back when I was broken and praying for a second chance.

Now, I was standing shoulder to shoulder with him.

Reading heart rhythms. As a nurse.

In that moment, it all came together—God placing the puzzle piece gently into its spot with a soft, perfect click.

Chapter 37:

Ghost of His Past

Sporadically, I'd visit Indy, but not often. My life had changed so much, and the city felt like an empty shell.

Levi's ghost was there, but only of his past. It wasn't his actual presence—the one filled with love and belonging. It was an echo, a trace of something once vibrant and alive.

I had our memories there, but without joy.

We'd shared such a concentrated time of love and passion—so intense it burned like fire through winter—but it passed. And now, I was only a hostage to my past.

I ached for his presence.

What I wouldn't give for one more deep conversation, one more touch, one more glance. I could still remember his scent, as if I'd hugged him that very morning before work. Earthy, clean, with a hint of musk that clung to my skin longer than it should have.

Unfortunately, the last time I caught that scent was years ago. Some experiences are so vivid and vibrant that they linger in your memory like a photograph that never fades. He was that vivid imagery for me.

I'd never felt freer and more alive in my life than I did when I was with him. Now, it felt like I had been in a coffin for years.

Would our love ever be resurrected?

As much as I desired it, I doubted it. There's never a happily-ever-after. That only happens in fairy tales. And my life certainly was not one.

As often as I'd let thoughts of Levi in, I'd cast them back out. They were too painful. They seemed hopeless.

And the love I experienced for him was so deep and tumultuous that I couldn't let it linger without hope. I wanted him back—but not how we had been.

It didn't just seem hopeless. It was hopeless.

Chapter 38:

A Season of Light

*I*n these early days of recovery, I spent my time doing things like preparing my daughter for her prom.

Mary reminds me of a porcelain doll—fair-skinned with that same striking strawberry blonde hair she'd had since she was little. That year, I took her to find the perfect dress. It was electric blue, with sequins embroidered into the top like tiny sparks of starlight. It shimmered under the boutique lights, just like her.

Her hair fell in waterfall curls streaming down her back, and her makeup was flawless, soft but radiant. She looked like she'd stepped out of a storybook. She posed proudly with her siblings that day—her delicate smile layered with strength and grace.

For a long time, she had taken on the mother role when I would not. Drugs take a person to a place where they can't carry out responsibilities. But the initial decision is just that—a choice. Making *can't* truly a *won't*.

Annie was becoming my little rainbow child. She was a social butterfly—laughing with friends, hosting slumber parties, creating endless pieces of art and imagination.

My favorite creation of hers during that time was a stop-motion video she made with Little People figurines and Jenga blocks. It told the story of the Tower of Babel, with an instrumental version of *Everybody Wants to Rule the World* playing in the background.

We worked on it together. I can still hear the clatter of blocks, the soft click of the camera, and the spark in her voice. I'll carry that memory with me forever.

My son was blossoming too. He wasn't speaking when I left—just making sounds or uttering one or two words. Though I cherished every noise he made, I yearned to hear him speak to me.

During this time, he began learning signs. He'd look at me with intent, shaping his fingers carefully, teaching me as he went. Never in a million years did I think my 4-year-old son would be teaching me sign language.

Then one beautiful day, he spoke.

It was the most beautiful sentence I'd ever heard in my life—all four words of it: *"I love you, Mom!"*

I whipped around, dropped to my knees in front of him, and hugged him so tight I probably squeezed the air out of his lungs. *"I love you too, Anthony,"* I whispered, blinking back tears.

From then on, he flourished like a forest after rain.

What amazed me most was his insight—especially into what God was speaking in the moment.

Later, after he'd begun speaking more, he surprised me again. I was regularly mentoring girls at the recovery center—teaching Bible study, leading classes, or simply offering time and presence.

One morning, as I prayed quietly, *"God, what would You have me do today?"* Anthony blurted out, *"Go to the Lighthouse and turn the light on!"*

I was stunned.

The Bible says, *"You are the light of the world..."* (Matthew 5:14).

So that day, I went and simply gave my presence to the girls.

As we drove away later, Anthony said, *"Well done."*

I instantly got chills—the kind you know come from the presence of the Lord if you've ever felt it.

"...Well done, my good and faithful servant! You have been faithful with a few things; I will put you in charge of many things. Come and share in your master's happiness."
—Matthew 25:21

God has certainly kept this promise.

Chapter 39:

The Plague

*A*las, life happens. A few years down the road, disaster struck again, as it tends to do.

There was a strange new illness that everyone seemed to be talking about or experiencing. At first, I didn't see it personally—not until it hit the facility where I was working.

The word was that this *plague* was killing people—lots of people.

Strangely enough, I didn't witness its effects until after the National Guard came in to administer the vaccine to staff and patients.

Just a couple of days later, one of my typically energetic and independent patients didn't get out of bed like he always did. He was an old postman—the kind who'd rise with the sun, sharp and punctual, even in his old age.

At first, I thought maybe it was a UTI or pneumonia—common culprits in the elderly, especially in nursing homes.

But then… others began falling ill. Laid out the same way.

Like dominoes tipped by invisible hands, they dropped—one after another.

Before I knew it, the sickness was sweeping through the entire facility.

Nobody was allowed inside except for the nurses. It was us against COVID-19.

I moved from room to room, heart pounding, breath fogging my face shield, just to check if my patients were still alive.

Each doorknob I touched felt like a roll of the dice. IV pumps beeped like a countdown.

Altogether, nearly half of the residents died during that first wave.

Being the nurse I am, I later signed up for a contract near Chicago and worked at a major hospital. The virus there was unforgiving.

I'll never forget one patient in particular. He was extremely grouchy—but I couldn't blame him. There was a framed picture in his room—him in a sharp suit, shaking hands with another businessman. He'd been a successful executive, standing tall in the prime of his life.

Now, he lay in that hospital bed, missing fingers and toes, his legs so swollen they looked like they might pop. His kidneys had mostly failed. His skin was pale and thin, and his eyes were heavy with exhaustion.

COVID had stolen his freedom, his independence, his identity.

I saw nothing but death and destruction during that season.

And there was nowhere to go for support. No place to pour it out.

So, again—I drank.

Chapter 40:

The Reaper

My habit returned with vengeance.

I could hear the inner me screaming, *"No, Prudence!"*—but it did no good. I opened the door wide and allowed its entrance into my life once again.

This was when divorce loomed heavy in the air—at least for me. My mental health was circling the drain, as it had several times before. I was miserable, and not just for one reason. I could point my finger at others, sure—but you know what they say about that: three more fingers pointing right back at me.

Finally, I admitted to Leroy that I wanted a divorce. He was calm and understanding about it, and I was broken and torn about my decision. Was I giving up too soon? I was devastated; I'm sure he was too. And then, I handled it terribly.

We'd made it through so much—things most couples never survive—but I just couldn't keep going. I think that was part of why I drank.

Memories of betrayal haunted me like ghosts clinging to the corners of my mind. It probably sounds like a lack of forgiveness, but it wasn't. I was just… done trying to be strong. I was broken, and I finally admitted it.

During this time, I began having intrusive, suicidal thoughts, like the grim reaper was looming around the corner. Every time I opened the med cart at work, I'd hear it—clear and deliberate in my mind:

"The next time, grab the fast-acting insulin and a syringe. Go to the bathroom. Inject the whole bottle. Lock the door so no one can get in to save you. You'll be gone before they can even try."

If it wasn't that exact thought, it was something just as dark. Each time I opened that cart—*"Grab the insulin and a syringe."*

Like clockwork. Like poison in a loop.

∼

Finally, one day at home, the most terrifying image popped into my mind—not just a flash, but an entire scene.

All at once, I saw myself hanging from the awning over the deck in the backyard. I saw my children—Mary, Annie, Anthony—discovering me.

That thought alone chilled me to the bone. I knew then that something had to change… or it would end me.

Chapter 41:

California Dreamin'

*B*efore I knew it, I was headed to rehab again—this time in California.

This is where I screamed in my sleep. A lot. I scared my roommates most nights. They'd ask me in the morning if I was okay, and I'd always say yes. But I wasn't.

There was one night my roommate had to wake me up just to keep me from tipping over my bedside table in a panic. The nightmares had that kind of grip.

I started that journey in what they call *wine country*, in a detox program in Murrieta, California. That's where I fell in love with Billie Eilish. Her voice felt like it knew me—aching and eerie. She sang me through my brokenness.

After detox, I trekked to San Diego for sober living. The house was in La Jolla, just two blocks from the Pacific Ocean. There was a rooftop sitting area at the top of the house, and I thought I must be in heaven. There were thin-trunked palms everywhere, and the ocean was a deep blue with white crests as the waves crashed against the rocks on the shore.

"All I had to do was admit I had a problem and ask for help?" I prayed. God was so good to me.

That program was incredible. I met a lot of amazing people there and basically lived in California for six months. I enjoyed everything about it—except that my children weren't there.

I loved the beach, the golden tan it gave me, and the illusion that I was a California girl. But I wasn't.

I was a Midwesterner at heart. Even the grocery store clerk knew. All I did was ask what aisle the *pop* was in.

"You're from the Midwest, aren't you?!" the clerk blurted out.

So, the first paycheck I got from my new nursing job—I was on my way back to Indiana.

The drive home was terrible. I had relapsed—again. A surfer boy from the program, who I'd spent a lot of time with during my stay, came with me. We made it to

New Mexico before he woke me in the middle of the night and asked me to take him to the airport.

I did.

When we got there, he said goodbye and got out.

The problem was… I didn't know the address of the hotel we'd been staying in.

"How do I get myself into these situations?" I thought, frustrated and exhausted.

When I finally made it back, I realized he'd stolen my laptop. I never saw or heard from him again.

It's things like that that make you realize how badly you don't want people like that in your life anymore.

Even so, I'm a firm believer: the things we go through are what shape us into who we're meant to be.

Chapter 42:

The Nest

I never anticipated the realization I'd come to when I returned home—The problem was, there was no home.

There was just a house. The one I used to share with my family.

The grand staircase still stood, but I'd never run up and down it again—at least not as part of that family. The windows were still large, letting sunshine pour into the living room—but I couldn't enjoy it anymore.

The walls looked the same, but they no longer held my elegant pictures or the vintage décor that gave the home its historical charm.

Instead, posters lined the walls. Two in particular stood out—one of Frankenstein, the other of Bill Murray in a scene from Kingpin.

Gross. I hated what was happening. I wasn't welcome to stay there anymore. I'm not sure why I thought I would be—after all, my husband and I were divorcing.

Then the devastation sank in like a stone in my gut: I wouldn't be living with my kids anymore.

He'd filed for sole physical custody, and I didn't contest it. I had no home. And after the relapse, I knew it was better for the kids.

They needed stability—and I barely had a place to lay my own head.

At the time, I was crammed into a sober living house with too many other women and not nearly enough space for peace.

It hadn't sunk in while I was away in California. But when I returned, the truth hit hard: I was an empty nester.

I hadn't realized, the day I left for detox, that it would be the last day I'd live with all three of my children.

I needed help badly, but I'm not sure I would have gone if I had known the cost. Even now, it brings burning tears to my eyes. My stomach aches just remembering it.

I'm sure a part of them felt like I didn't love them anymore. But how untrue that is.

Maybe, at times, the best thing I could do for them was to remove myself—to stop being a negative influence.

Still… I wish I could have done more. Stayed longer. Been stronger.

I don't know if I'll ever truly make peace with it.

Eventually, I got a three-bedroom house with a friend I'd met in sober living. She was amazing, and we shared the same goals. Once we settled in, Anthony started coming every other weekend.

I made up a beautiful room for the girls. They never came to spend the night.

I don't blame them. But it broke my heart.

I wish I'd been more stable. More trustworthy. I'm still learning how to be that for them today. It's a constant work in progress—and I have to give my brokenness to God daily.

But without their company… without their voices filling the house…

The sadness settled in. The loneliness was deafening.

And soon, yearning for connection— I went looking in all the wrong places.

A Letter to My Children

My Dear Children,

There are no words big enough to contain the love I feel for you — but I will try.

You are my heart.

Every single day, in ways I can never fully explain, you are with me. In my thoughts. In my prayers. In the way I move through the world. Even in the darkest times — and you've seen me walk through many — my love for you never faded. Not once. Even when I was lost, even when I was broken, even when I couldn't show up the way you needed me to, you were always the reason I wanted to find my way back.

I know I hurt you. I know I wasn't always the mother you needed, and I carry that grief with me. It lives in the quiet spaces — the birthdays I missed, the nights I wasn't there, the confusion I caused. I would give anything to undo those moments. If I could gather them up in my hands and rewrite them, I would. But I can't.

So instead, I write to you now with all the truth I have: I am sorry. I am so deeply, endlessly sorry.

But I also want you to know this — I got better.

I fought. I scraped my way out of the darkness. I faced myself and chose to keep going because I wanted to be the woman you could be proud of. I wanted to be the mom you deserved. And I'm still becoming her — every single day.

Today, I live a life of purpose. I work hard. I stay clean. I show up. I talk to God — a lot. And every victory, every quiet night, every smile, every breath of peace... I owe it to Him and to you.

You have taught me what it means to hope. To grow. To love without limits.

You didn't ask for this story — and yet you were caught in it. I wish I could shield you from the scars, but what I can do now is live in a way that helps you heal, too. I want to earn your trust — not just once, but every single day forward. I want to show you that people can change. That love can outlast pain. That God can rebuild what we shatter.

I will never stop loving you. I will never stop praying for you. I will never stop trying.

Thank you for being my reason to keep going. Thank you for being part of my healing — even if you didn't know you were. You are the greatest gift I have ever been given.

With all my love, always,
Mom

Chapter 43:

Narcissistic Hoosier

*M*en. I had daddy issues, so I was immediately on the prowl for a man.

I found myself on a dating site and met my next mistake—Jacob. The first time I saw him, I wondered if he was sick. He was so thin his cheekbones looked hollow, his arms like twigs under a wrinkled T-shirt. But he seemed nice enough. He took me to dinner and told me all about himself—that he was a Marine, a fireman, and a father. He seemed like what we Midwesterners call a *good ole boy*. "*I'm getting a little old to be picky about looks,*" I thought to myself. So, we continued dating.

We dated for about three months before I moved in with him, and six months before we were married. We had my son record the *ceremony* at the courthouse. First, I had to get drunk to say yes, because Jacob bugged me about it so much. Second, you could still see how freaked out I was in the video as we stood there getting married. It was all over my face—stiff smile, eyes darting. I didn't want to do it.

The entire marriage was ill-fitting from the start. He was emotionally abusive and used fear tactics to keep me in a constant state of anxiety, so I'd stay.

There was a time when we'd both gone to an overturned semi accident. When he asked me to go, I should've said no—but I didn't. The scene was traumatic. Shards of glass and twisted metal scattered the road. I watched the driver die as they worked to pull him from the cab without success. Later that night, I wanted to talk about it—I was shaking inside, like my nerves had turned to ice—but Jacob avoided me. He seemed emotionally void, like nothing had happened.

I continued to plead with him, hoping he would eventually talk to me, hold me, or offer some kind of comfort. But he didn't.

Finally, he jumped up and out of bed. I followed him, still begging him to stay and be there with me through this, but he refused.

That was when I finally gave up. *"I can't be with someone who can't even sit and talk with me through a traumatic experience they knowingly took me to,"* I said to him, *"I'm going to my mom's in the morning."*

This happened on August 25, 2022. I had gone to bed. It was about 3 a.m. when I heard it, pounding on the back screen door.

I was in my pajamas—no bra—when I got up, heart hammering, to see what was happening.

As I entered the dining room, I saw an officer in uniform, his hand hovering near his holster.

He shouted, *"You have the right to remain silent…"*

I froze in shock. *"For what?!"* I asked.

"You know what!" the cop hissed.

I looked at Jacob, but his face was blank. Empty. Not a flicker of surprise or concern. Just stone.

From then on, I felt trapped. I was found to be completely innocent and received no charges, but I spent a few nights in a holding cell. For what? I never received any real answer.

The significance of that date was crushing. Since it had passed midnight, it was Mary's 21st birthday—and

I couldn't even tell her happy birthday on one of the most special days of her life.

I was in jail again, and I knew she would never believe I hadn't done anything wrong. Ever. She'd already experienced so much trauma from my past that trying to explain it would only sound like shirking responsibility.
Maybe it was.

Later, I realized my part in all of it: I'd chosen to be with someone for no good reason. Someone irresponsible and emotionless. Someone I knew wasn't meant for me.

Chapter 44:

No Joke

This was all happening during my FNP program (which was about the only good thing I was doing at that time).

There were assignments due almost every day of the week. It was required to log in at least every other day. I spent that time wondering if I had allowed a person into my life who would destroy it without batting an eye.

It sure felt that way.

It took a long time and many tries, but I finally left Jacob for good—on his birthday. It was November 3, 2024. I think I did that on purpose, so it would feel cruel if he never considered trying to rekindle things.

I've never met a more imposturous person in my life. He'd fooled me completely.

Strangely enough, I had initially left him on April 1, 2024. It wasn't planned that way, but it turned into a kind of *Joke's on you* moment.

Exactly one year later, on April 1, 2025, Jacob died of a heart attack.

You can't even make this stuff up.

Looking back, I can see that God was sparing me from a huge mess.

Even so, I still feel like the heartache and stress our relationship caused him may have been a contributing factor in his death.

Being 100% honest, I feel God partially allowed that to happen, so I would never consider going back.

The reason I believe this is because there were a few times after I left him the first time that I did. I went and came back several times. My mind felt fickle, confused.

Chapter 45:

As Good as Gone

I was married, but I was miserable. If I'd thought more deeply before this, I may have known it was coming.

Jacob was a rebound as much as I hate to admit it. I'd been, yet again, trying to drink myself to death. My husband wouldn't work; he'd sent me to jail by lying to the police, and I felt afraid and trapped.

Everything around me looked grim. Everything was dead—including me—on the inside.

I'll never forget the day… it was March 22, 2024. As I'd done so many times before, I opened Facebook to scroll mindlessly. I needed something to distract me from my misery.

As I looked at my phone screen, my heart almost leapt out of my throat.

It had been ten years since we'd spoken. He liked my reel. *"Is this for real?!"* I asked myself. I hadn't felt such relief and excitement in years.

It was Levi. He was alive.

I'd long ago given up the idea that he'd get clean. In fact, I was pretty certain he had overdosed and died by now. If that was the case, I definitely didn't want to know, so I'd stopped looking him up.

But here he was.

I clicked on his name to scan his page, and I was shocked.

He had been using Facebook as a journal of his accomplishments since getting out of prison.

"Please, God, don't let this be a drug-fueled manifesto!" I prayed.

He described his life now: he was in college with a high GPA, sober, and helping to manage a sober living house.

He looked fantastic.

I was in heaven.

I knew in that moment I was as good as gone. I was leaving my husband—and quickly. Suddenly, vines and flowers began growing like a garden inside my heart.

Hope was restored.

I went to send him a message and a friend request.

He was still active!

I could not wait to hear back from him.

Chapter 46:

Paradoxical

I sent him a message, but to my disappointment, he soon became inactive. I was sad, but I was encouraged. He went to sleep. His page couldn't be a drug-fueled manifesto. He sleeps now. I couldn't wait until the next morning. That night seemed to last forever. I needed to hear from him soon. I was dying inside, and I was certain his re-entry into my life would bring me back to life.

This couldn't have come at a better time. I'd been living in a narcissistic rebound relationship where I was drinking myself to death. I was desperately trying to stay sane as I navigated the FNP program. I was almost done—if I could just make it to the finish line. It seemed impossible… until Levi showed up.

The next morning came, and there was his message! I wish I could tell you what it said, but I can't even remember. I skimmed through his words as though I was scanning his very body in my presence. This was really happening, and I hadn't been so hopeful and excited at the same time in years.

I had been speaking to him, but I hadn't seen him—yet. Believe me, that was going to happen. I know, I know… I was married. But if you'd been in that relationship, having experienced the reality Levi and I shared all those years ago, I promise you, you'd give it another shot. Levi was the best version of himself I'd ever seen—through pictures and professions, anyway.

Finally, one night, Jacob and I had been fighting all night, yet again, and I'd had it. I asked Levi to please meet me to give me gas money. What I don't think he realized was that the gas money was just so I could refill my tank to the point it had been when I left my house to see him. I had become what they call "broke, busted, and disgusted," and thankfully, Levi didn't care.

We met. It was at Walmart. I pulled in, so nervous. I'd been waiting for this moment for ten years. I thought all hope was lost. Then this.

There he was. Calm. Sweet. Rested. Inviting. His green eyes—the same as they had been 10 years ago. His hair was no longer buzzed. He had length to his hair. It was a soft brown. I wanted to touch it, but I waited. The time would come.

He appeared sane, peaceful, and humane. He reminded me of the passage where the demons were tormenting a man. Demons possessed him. Then one day, Jesus casts them out. The man comes into town, sane and in his right mind, and it scares the townspeople (Luke 8:26-39). This is how I felt. His sanity was so out of character for him that his transformation seemed paradoxical. Only God could be responsible for such a miracle.

Levi and I were meant for one another. I truly feel God healed him for me. I know that sounds selfish, but you must understand: I know he has a bigger purpose. My statement comes from a place of relationship with God. He knew how badly I grieved Levi and saw how hard I even tried to move on. I never could forget him.

Chapter 47:

Walmart Parking Lot

*H*e stood at the gas pump in khakis and a nice winter coat, dressed in casual boots. He looked so tall and handsome. The old, familiar feeling of safety and belonging lingered in his presence, just as it had before. I hugged him with all that I had within me, I breathed in his same, familiar scent as if it were the oxygen I'd been missing for a decade. I didn't want to let go. It was the best feeling I'd felt since we'd touched all those years ago. He looked good with meat on his bones. He was almost—stocky. I liked it.

We spoke a few nervous words. But I knew I was going to have many more, and we weren't going to be separating that day. We soon found ourselves sitting in his Pontiac G6. We sat in his warm little sporty ride, and I enjoyed it so much. I looked at him without hesitation. It was as if our eye contact was a kiss. I immediately held his hand. He looked at me with those sweet, puppy-dog-like eyes.

"Is this really happening?" Levi said. My heart skipped a beat.

Levi was becoming the man I'd always hoped for. Sober, intelligent, steady, calm, reasonable, and definitely sexy. He wore glasses now, and I thought it so adorable when he pushed them back up and off his nose. His writing was to die for. I thought back to an earlier conversation between us through text.

I was struggling in clinical, and he randomly wrote to me. I'd long ago fallen back into a pit of despair. He wrote the most beautiful encouragement letter I think I'd ever received. As I read it, I realized Levi wasn't putting on a front. He had done the inner work. I could sense from the moment I read his words that God had sent him to help me out of my mess. He was the very last person I thought would be capable of such a thing. Yet, here we sat.

We continued to speak that day in the Walmart parking lot. He'd been doing real things—managing a sober living facility, raising awareness for a local homeless man whose house had burned down. He had drawn enough attention that the house was built entirely free for the man. Levi was living a repentant life.

His efforts had even been published in People Magazine.

This is the stuff of dreams. I often thought, How can this be? He was here. He was healthy. And just as I felt the first time we met, he was mine.

It was eight short days later that I left my abusive, narcissistic relationship and moved into a shelter. It was there that I finished my master's degree—clean and sober. I was living there when I graduated from the FNP program, but I made it.

I firmly believe that if you don't have to sacrifice anything to get it, it isn't worth getting. I gave everything I had, and I made it—barely. Just as I was finishing my program, he resurfaced in my life, and I was elated. My college graduation was the stuff of dreams. It was me, my mom, and my love who were present that day. To me, less is more. In times like that, the people who really love you and care about you will show up.

Interlude: Embers to Flames

"I keep these longings locked
In lowercase inside a vault
Someone told me
There's no such thing as bad thoughts
Only your actions talk
These fatal fantasies
Giving way to labored breath
Taking all of me
We've already done it in my head
If it's make-believe
Why does it feel like a vow?
We'll both uphold somehow?
They don't know how you've haunted me
So stunningly

I choose you and me
... Religiously"

I couldn't have said it better than Taylor Swift sang it.
I was... always, guilty as sin.

The desire for my other half never died. It was a burning
ember I had to shelter from the wind, so it wouldn't ignite
into wildfire—within me, and all around me.

HEROINE

"What if he's written 'mine' on my upper thigh
Only in my mind?"

Taylor sings…

He had—the moment we met—and I've worn it since. I've always been his.

There was a time I had to let the desire die, or it would kill me. And just as the entire garden had withered and browned, the rain came.

It felt cold and wet and fitting—death, rain, boredom, sadness… the silence after a storm that never stops. But then—the sun broke through.

At first, it burned my eyes. I couldn't see anything. I had been engulfed in the dark for so long. But quickly, my eyes adjusted.

And I saw—the garden coming to life again. The grass turned green. Flower buds pushed up through the soil. Then, the colors burst: irises, sunflowers, daffodils, peonies, roses— all blooming in unison, releasing a fragrance I will never forget.

Suddenly, a man walked toward me through the garden. Tall. Handsome. Steady.

CHASTIDY MADER

To my complete and utter surprise, it was the love of my life.

*At once, the wind blew and the flames roared all around us.
The fire engulfed us—and everything else. No more sadness.
No more wondering, waiting, or hiding.*

*The embers were fanned by the wind, and we were on fire—
once again.*

*Our love had covered a multitude of sins.
God had plucked the most hidden, deep, scandalous desire
from my heart—and made it a masterpiece for the world to
behold.*

*The time had come—as we so desired—He displayed us for
the world to see.
Miracles do happen, after all.*

Chapter 48:

Pillow Talk

*A*round that magical time, we decided to try it again. We were healthy now. We were completely different people, but still very much in love. When we touched, it was as if the embrace had never been gone. We picked up where we left off—only without the drugs and lifestyle we'd lived a decade ago.

I will never forget the first night we spent together. He was staying at a beautiful hotel in Indy for training at his new job as a rehab tech. He invited me to stay with him, and I did. It isn't what you think—we didn't sleep with each other. Believe me, though, I wanted to.

Instead, we had pillow talk, snacks, and cuddles as waves played softly in the background. It felt so right. It felt... well, perfect, to be honest. The next morning, we awoke and ventured downstairs to eat. We picked through a variety of breakfast foods, laughing and leaning into the comfort of the moment.

It was surreal.

I heard instrumental music playing in the background, but didn't recognize it at first. Not until we were heading back to our table in that fancy dining room. Then it hit me— *Don't You (Forget About Me)* was playing.

God answered my question from ten years ago. Levi hadn't forgotten about me.

In the beginning, we bickered—a lot. We broke up— a lot. We cried—a lot. Was this truly meant to be? Was I going to take this seriously? Could I? How is that even possible after everything we'd been through a decade ago?

The more time I spent around Levi, the more I realized I was sicker than he was. I continued to drink— on and off. Finally, one night, my mental health took another downward spiral. I think it was all the back and forth I'd done trying to separate from my then-husband, Jacob. He was a narcissist, and he would love-bomb me—and I'd fall for it again and again.

As I mentioned before, I did finally leave him for good, but I was a mess. I again decided to stop drinking, and in that, I had the worst withdrawal symptoms of my life. I didn't want to be alive anymore.

I told Levi that.He listened.

For what seemed like two weeks straight, I lay in bed, frozen in fear. I had anxiety so bad in the pit of my stomach that I thought I would explode. Any noise made me angry. I even told Levi to stop breathing so hard.

He would respond gently, *"I'm sorry, baby. I love you."* He would look at me with those kind, steady eyes.

As far as I can remember, he lay there with me as I detoxed and suffered by my own hand and decisions. THAT is love, my friend.

Never in a million years would I have imagined Levi as the healing balm of Christ, but here he was—as just that.

Chapter 49:

Official

*I*t was November 28, 2024, that I made our relationship public. He deserved it. He shouldn't have had to "earn" it, but if there was a way to do that, he did it. I was so excited for him to see it. I was so proud that it was true.

He was my prince. God had really done all of this. I was finally accepting the impossible truth.

Later that year, we traveled to South Florida for vacation. If I thought I was in love before, I had no idea what love even was. We fell into such a deep level of love that I knew I never wanted to live another day without him in it.

There were so many special moments while we were there. One day that stands out was when we were scheduled to go snorkeling in the Keys. We got up and got ready that morning, but there was an error. The location wasn't where we thought it was, so the entire day had to be rescheduled—and I'm so incredibly glad it did.

That day, we ended up in Sanibel. We lay on the sandy beach together, hearing the waves crash and feeling the sun on our faces, which was wonderful to us because there was snow on the ground at home.

I'd been on these Captiva cruises in the past, and they were quaint and quite enjoyable. I scheduled a sunset cruise for Levi and me in Captiva. After an afternoon soaking up the sun, we ate dinner and headed to the harbor for our cruise.

The weather couldn't have been more perfect. We boarded the two-story cruise boat with a few others and proceeded out into the waters. The breeze blew through our hair, the sun kissed our noses, and dolphins jumped joyfully around the boat.

It was the stuff of dreams.

Levi smiled like a child. It touched my heart to see such innocent joy on his face. It made him even more handsome. We stared at one another a lot that evening. I was finally seeing him for the miraculous man he'd become, and I was head over heels in love.

I was never letting this man go again.

We hugged, cuddled, smiled, kissed, and posed for sunset pictures. It was like a dream. It felt like a honeymoon—only we weren't married... yet.

Chapter 50:

Prayer Whispers

*T*hank you, God. Thank you so much," Levi whispered. *"You're so beautiful,"* he continued softly. *"Thank you for giving me this chance, God."*

I was only half awake—just enough to hear him talking. My heart swelled. He was thanking God... and complimenting me... all while I lay beside him in the early hours of the morning.

Who is this? I wondered.

"I love you so much," I whispered.

"I love you too, Prudence," he poured back.

Was this really our life now? Had we come so far that God Himself had pieced us back together after all we'd done?

It felt real. It was real.

We were clean. Sober. We even went to church together.

I was trying to pass my board certification. And Levi... he was working at a recovery center. From what I heard, he was a true inspiration to the men he served.

I was lying next to a man of God.

God had heard the cry of my heart—and He couldn't take it anymore. So He healed us... and brought me back to Levi.

Since when was Levi a man of God? Since when was he a recovery coach? An advocate for the voiceless? On the board of a movement for the homeless and addicted?

Since now.

"This is really happening," I whispered to myself. *"Thank You, God,"* I breathed in prayer. *"You heard me."*

Chapter 51:

Marry Me

On one of our last evenings there, we headed to Fort Myers Beach to catch the sunset. The sunset was gorgeously romantic. After it ended, we walked hand in hand to get ice cream. As we exited with our cones, Lover by Taylor Swift played in the streets.

That was an absolute God moment because that song had meant a lot to us both—Taylor had pretty much sung the entire soundtrack of our lives, in order. She even sang for the times when we were apart.

We walked down the road to explore, but not for long—it was getting dark and chilly. It was December, after all, and we were right next to the water.

As we approached another section of the beach, strange lights were sitting in the sand. We got closer.

The letters read: **MARRY ME.**

Levi looked at me. I knew he was asking me then, although I somewhat rejected the moment, which I regret immensely. God had orchestrated that moment. I knew in my heart we were to be married.

That night we made love.

He kissed me with the passion of Romeo. His fingers gently slid under my shirt, up my torso, and to my breasts. He tugged my nipples, and I was instantly ready for him.

He knelt and leaned in. His fingers opened the petals of the flower, one with a sweet, succulent nectar. He pressed his tongue into the drink. I could barely breathe. I let out a gentle cry of pleasure as I grasped his hair. Our eyes met, and he returned to me for a wet kiss. It was as if our clothes simply dropped to the floor.

His penetration took my breath away. Our bodies were meant for one another. He stared into my soul as he invaded my space.

"I love you," he said.

Our breath was heavy, his thrusts becoming more pleasurable to me with each one. Then, there was a splash of ultimate joy between us. Incredible. Unheard of. That was us.

That is still us.

Chapter 52:

Snake in the Garden

We came home refreshed and more in love than ever before. We were floating on cloud nine. Life felt wonderful—until one Sunday morning, when I received a long message from a woman Levi had previously worked with while helping her and her husband open a sober living facility. She had become a confidant during a difficult time, and he had confided in her about my drinking issues and the emotional back-and-forth between him and my husband. He had been understandably hurt and said some things. I'm sure he just needed someone to talk to, but...

The message began, *"I know you think he's your Prince Charming, but..."*

My heart dropped into my stomach. I got dizzy. My lungs tightened like they'd been kicked. I couldn't breathe.

"Levi is a snake. He talks about you like you don't follow guidelines," she wrote. *"This is why I can't have you work*

for us. I want to be as morally sound as possible. But keep doing what you're doing — you're a beacon of hope for many!"

My skin flushed hot. My ears buzzed.

"First of all," I thought, *"if you see my relationship thriving and feel compelled to sabotage it, YOU are the snake."*

People say things they don't mean when they're upset.

I had gone back and forth between Jacob and Levi many times — torn between confusion and the desire to do the right thing. I would ask myself: *Do I honor the commitment I made — even if it was made while drunk? Or do I acknowledge that the relationship was toxic and dangerous to my future?* I truly wanted to make the right decision. It seems obvious now, but it didn't then.

Levi had been hurt when he said whatever it was that he said. I know he was.

Still, I messaged him at work to tell him what had happened. He responded immediately, full of remorse. I could feel his humility — even his fear — knowing I now knew what he'd said, no matter the reason.

I remained calm, but I was wounded.

"Can he manage his emotions in difficult situations?" I wondered.

He didn't say a cross word the rest of the day. I think he could feel the state of my heart.

That evening, he came home to the apartment. We sat down to talk. I was surprisingly composed.

"How dare you say anything that could jeopardize what I've worked so hard to rebuild! I don't care how mad, sad, or hurt you were!" I hissed, fury coiled inside me. *"After this stunt, I have to seriously consider whether we can continue. I have to trust the people I let close to me. You know what I'm risking. Jacob wasn't safe for me—or the life I'm trying to live—and you know that."*

"I know," he said quietly.

He sat completely still. His eyes showed fear—and I felt he should be scared. I was seriously considering walking away.

The truth was, I practiced within strict guidelines—maybe obsessively so because of my past. I never came close to crossing a line. The fact that the DEA even gave me a license after all I'd been through was a miracle. I wasn't going to risk it. Not now. Not ever.

God had entrusted me with much, and I planned to steward it with integrity.

He sat across from me, his eyes heavy with shame. I could feel the remorse in the air. His spirit was downcast.

Then suddenly, he pulled off his glasses and rubbed his eyes.

"I don't care what it is," he said. *"I just want you to be my girlfriend."*

My heart softened. I got up, walked to his side of the table, and wrapped my arms around him tightly.

"OK," I said. *"But don't you EVER say anything like that again. If it happens again, it's over. Immediately."*

He agreed. I felt the weight fall off him.

I wanted him just as much—maybe even more—than he wanted me. We were going to have to make this work.

Chapter 53:

My (Pre) Valentine

*A*s time passed, we continued to grow closer. Sometimes, it's the challenges that cause people to persevere—and thankfully, that was the case for us. We worked things out for a few weeks, but then we got into it again and broke up.

It was sad. Really, really sad.

But it didn't last long.

I missed him too much. It was like I couldn't live without him. Not in any healthy way, anyway.

True to my nature, I'm a sucker for escape, and I had planned another trip to Florida in April. I had intended to go alone, but the minute we made up, I invited him to come with me.

That changed everything.

On February 12th, 2025, Levi drove me to Indianapolis for my evening shift. He dropped me off for work and went to run errands.

I was really doing this. I was working as a nurse practitioner.

I remember, when I was in the thick of addiction and homelessness, if you had told me I'd be in this position, I would have laughed in your face. But now, I was walking with my head held high.

These days, I love to dress up and wear heels. I used to loathe what I call *clackers*, and now I am one. Maybe it was simply because I was jealous, but now I don't have to be. So, I clack away in my heels down the hallways of my workplace.

There was a time I couldn't even take care of myself. Now I was taking care of others.

When he returned, there was a bag by the gearshift. It looked fancy.

"Are you going to open it?" he asked.

I was nervous. Surely this wasn't a ring—not yet. I reached into the bag. It was a jewelry box. Don't get too excited, Prudence, I warned myself.

I lifted the lid. It was a ring. A beautiful, sparkling diamond ring.

I don't remember what I said at first—I was in shock.

"Well?" he asked.

"Yes! You know I'll marry you!" I exclaimed.

Chapter 54:

Barefoot

*L*evi had forgotten his shoes—but I was ok with that.

I looked down at my manicured toes in the sand. My white sundress whipped gently in the breeze. The day was cloudy, but I didn't mind. It felt like us—a little overcast, but still warm. Still full of beauty.

At once, my eyes were drawn to the shoreline.

There he was. My fiancé.

He looked so handsome—white button-down, khaki shorts, barefoot like me. He stood close to the edge of the water, and I began to march through the sand to meet him.

The wind was at my back. The clouds shielded the sun, but the air was perfect. Fresh. Like our life together was about to be.

He was my knight in shining armor. My prince. My love.

Forever, I would never let him go again.

That day, he was to be my husband.

We read our personally crafted vows aloud—we are writers, after all. Our ceremony included the reading of 1 Corinthians 13. This time, the list described our love; how it is today.

The breeze was cool, and it was only us—an elopement.

We exchanged gazes. I think we both wondered, Is this really happening?

We looked shyly, innocently, and soberly at one another—no longer needing to remove a veil of fear.

It was true. It was real.

And I know we both couldn't wait to see what would come next.

Chapter 55:

Rewriting Nursing Culture

*E*very single day I wake up, I'm still in awe of what God has done in my life. Sometimes I just sit with it—stunned. I shouldn't be here. But I am. And to top it all off, I now teach at the very college I graduated from over 20 years ago. It's surreal. I light up when I teach. I feel alive in the classroom. My students give me so much hope. I find myself tearing up on my way home from teaching—often.

Sometimes I look around and think, *How did I end up in such a dark place all those years ago?* I've spent a lot of time trying to understand it.

For far too long, nurses have worn a badge of honor for not taking care of themselves. Skipping lunch breaks, holding their bladders for entire shifts, going 12 hours without so much as a sip of water—these things have become normalized. And if a nurse does manage to sneak a bite or a drink, they're often reprimanded for having it at the nurse's station. The truth is, they're just trying to keep up—just trying to survive the day with some small reserve of energy.

It's heartbreaking. And it's dangerous.

For years, nurses were physically and verbally assaulted without consequence. And while some progress has been made, the culture of nursing still desperately needs change. I can't let go of this idea. It keeps coming back to me. I think it's because, deep down, I know this very culture played a role in my own unraveling.

When the job teaches you, day after day, that your basic needs don't matter—eventually, you believe it, and when you believe you don't matter, you stop trying to take care of yourself. That lie was one of the seeds of my addiction. I was seeking relief, and I found it where I could—whenever I could.

I'm not a political person. I never have been. But I do believe in change—real, meaningful change. And I know where it starts. It starts in the classroom. It starts with the next generation of nurses.

That's why I pour myself into my students. That's why I say things like: *"Take your lunch break." "Step off the unit." "Take that trip." "Go to that event." "Pick up that hobby."*

Because these aren't just words. They're lifelines. They're lessons I learned the hard way.

Nursing is one of the most stressful, demanding careers out there. We carry so much. We give so much. But we can't keep pouring from an empty cup. We can't care for others when we don't even care for ourselves.

I lost a lot to learn that truth. But now, I'm using it to plant something better.

Chapter 56:

Three Tears and a Testimony

*T*oday, I work as a nurse practitioner. But don't get it twisted—I still face real challenges.

I didn't pass my board certification on the first try. When I found out, I let myself cry exactly three tears. Then I got in my car and drove to work that evening.

I hadn't planned to tell anyone. But God had other plans.

A nurse—also in recovery—was nearby, talking about how hard it was to pass boards. I wasn't even part of the conversation, but I turned around and joined in. And in that small moment, God used a fellow traveler to begin healing something in me.

I hated that I didn't pass, but something inside reignited.

A flame. A fight. I hadn't come this far to stop now.

I studied for a month straight—even at work. The next time, I took the ANCC exam—and passed.

The first time, I'd taken the AANP because I'd heard it was the easier one. But a week after passing the ANCC, I went back and retook the AANP—and passed that one too.

Now, I'm a double-board-certified nurse practitioner.

If I hadn't failed the first time, I wouldn't be able to say that.

And I have to admit—it feels really good to say it.

Chapter 57:

The Alexander View

Staying in recovery is a battle.

You don't become a homeless meth-and-heroin needle junkie overnight—and you sure as hell don't come back from it overnight either.

Sometimes you take it one moment at a time. Other times, the days fly by—and they actually feel good.

These days, when I'm doing things that support my recovery—like working out at the Irsay YMCA—I sometimes glance across at The Alexander and its blown-glass lanterns.

Back in the day, when Levi and I were lost in addiction, I used to stare at those lights and wish I had a reason to stay there. I craved normalcy. I just wanted to feel like I belonged somewhere clean.

Years later, when I ran the Indy Mini Marathon, I stayed at The Alexander.

It was symbolic. I had once run these streets chasing a high. Now, I was running them for victory.

I challenged myself—and proved what I was capable of when I committed.

You have to control your mind. Don't let your mind control you.

To be victorious, you don't have to be perfect. You have to be **authentic**.

Fear doesn't disappear—it lingers. But the difference between people who rise and people who don't is this: Victorious people show up **in spite** of fear.

The others stay home—still afraid—and do nothing.

I'd rather show up shaking and be called **victorious** than hide in comfort and be called a **coward**.

So here I am—passing the torch.

Now **you** can be called victorious, too.

Reflection:

Somewhere Between Grit and Grace

There's a space between ruin and redemption nobody talks about.

It's not the moment you hit rock bottom. It's not the day you walk out of rehab with a plastic bag of belongings.

It's everything that comes after.

The grind. The quiet. The voice in your head saying, *"This isn't worth it."*

I thought falling apart was the worst thing. But rebuilding from nothing?

That's worse.

Nobody tells you how quiet the world gets when the chaos stops. How loud your thoughts become when you're no longer numb.

How lonely it feels when the ones who ran the streets with you disappear—and the ones you hurt aren't ready to forgive you.

I stood in that space with no applause. No high. No dope. No man on my arm.

Just me. And God.

And I learned that real strength isn't surviving hell.

It's choosing not to go back.

It's handing your past to God with trembling hands and saying, *"Do something with this wreckage."*

I made mistakes I'll never outrun. Burned bridges I may never rebuild. Ran from people who loved me. Ran toward people who used me.

And yet... Grace found me anyway.

Not because I earned it.

But because that's what grace does.

I don't have a fairytale ending.

What I have is better.

I have my integrity back.

I have a God who stayed when everyone else left.

And I have the guts to say: This is not who I was. This is who I choose to be.

Chapter 58:

Trauma & True

*T*here was undoubtedly a time when Levi and I shared a trauma bond. But let me be clear—my addiction was mine. We fell into darkness together, yes, but I didn't spiral because of him. I chose that path. Over and over, Levi asked if we could stop and work on becoming a healthy couple. He said yes. I said no. Again, he said yes. Again, I said no.

I didn't believe it was possible. But he showed me otherwise.

We spent ten years apart—ten years focused on healing. Levi spent more time in prison, but while he was there, he did the inner work. He often speaks of his moment of clarity—the fear that he would never change. That he'd stay the man he had been.

And then he surrendered.

Meanwhile, I let God sanctify me and refresh my spirit. I found my worth again—in Him. When Levi and I reunited, he had been clean and sober for over six years. I had logged years of sobriety, too, although I'd relapsed on alcohol here and there. But when we found each other again, Levi wanted nothing to do with my old habits.

He could have used my drinking as an excuse to fall back into our past. But he didn't.

Instead, he lay beside me while I detoxed—while I spewed negativity, fear, and shame. He met it with nothing but love and prayer. He didn't flinch. He didn't run. He stayed.

He reminded me who I was without substances. He helped me remember the woman I had been before.

And every morning—every single morning—I wake up to his prayers over me.

God picked Levi up, turned him around, and placed him on solid ground. Maybe God knew how deeply I loved him. Perhaps He knew I would never be truly fulfilled until I experienced love the way Levi loves me now.

For that, I will always be grateful.

What once began as a trauma bond is now something sacred. Something whole. True love.

What began in trauma became a testimony. Our love survived because it transformed—just like we did.

Chapter 59:

My Life Today

(And My Advice to You)

*T*oday, I work as a nurse practitioner, Monday through Friday. On Wednesdays, I teach nursing students at the same college I graduated from over two decades ago.

In the evenings, I sit beside Levi. Desks side by side. We often sit in silence together, keys clicking, as our souls seemingly dance in the peace we long ago hoped for.

Sometimes I'm typing a progress note. Sometimes, a word of encouragement to a student is all that's needed. And sometimes…a story like this one.

I live in victory now. But my life is normal.

We bicker like everyone else. We fight and make up.

I still face fear and anxiety—but they don't own me anymore.

Any day I live clean and sober is a thousand times better than my best day on drugs.

I have a relationship with all my kids. I love them more than words. Some days, I wonder if I hurt them too much—if I crossed a line that can't be undone.

But they keep letting me in. They keep trusting me a little more.

And I'm just so grateful to be here—alive, sober, and able to listen, love, and offer sound advice.

I'm now a daughter my mother can be proud of. A sister worth looking up to.

And my greatest aim? To inspire others... and to never stop inspiring myself.

I thank God every single day for healing me. Without Him, none of this would be possible.

Life is romantic and exciting. It's also scary and sad.

You've got to take the good with the bad—because life will give you both.

If I could leave you with anything, it would be this: Feel the feelings. Do it even when you're afraid. And never believe that something is beyond your reach.

Because with God, it isn't.

Present yourself to Him. Fully. Honestly. Trembling if you must.

And He will take you places you never dreamed possible.

With love, In Christ, Chastidy Mader

Chapter 60:

Epilogue – The Lanterns

*T*wilight was fitting. The weather was perfect, which was strange with it being early August.. Across the table sat my sweetheart, Levi. He looked incredibly handsome—I'd never seen him in a suit and tie before. But all I could focus on were his tender, hunter green eyes. It didn't matter what he wore. His being clean and sober was the most beautiful thing I'd ever seen him in.

His hair was slicked back neatly. His smile was so gentle. His ears always wiggle, his lips lightly touch, and his cheeks lift when his smile is completely genuine—when he's smitten with me in the moment.

Then, the music began.

The drum tapped. The trumpet shrilled. The sound poured into the air like honey. A tribute to Frank Sinatra. It was perfect. I'd been listening to the *Fifty Shades of Grey* soundtrack lately, and suddenly, the vocalist stepped to the microphone: *"Those fingers in my hair, That sly come-hither stare, That strips my conscience bare — It's witchcraft."*

Wow. To hear it live… It must be a dream.

I gazed around us in wonder. And just then — they caught my eye.

The lanterns.

The lanterns of The Alexander Hotel.

I guess we did belong here, after all.

Looking Back: Heroine

I never set out to become a cautionary tale.

But I also never imagined I'd survive the things I did.

Looking back, I can finally see that every chapter—the heartbreak, the betrayal, the addiction, the jail cells, the near-death moments—was writing a story I hadn't yet understood.

A story I had to live before I could tell.

For years, I chased love, acceptance, and worth in all the wrong places. I tried to numb the ache with needles, pills, men, work, even good things like family and faith.

But nothing stuck. Because healing doesn't come from chasing, it comes from surrendering.

I had to lose everything—my freedom, my dignity, my sanity—before I found the one thing I had been searching for all along:

Grace.

Not the kind you earn by being good enough. Not the type you barter for with half-hearted promises.

The kind that meets you in the gutter, wraps you in mercy, and whispers: You're still Mine.

Today, I stand on the other side of that nightmare. Not because I fought my way out.

But because I finally stopped fighting the One who'd been chasing me all along.

I'm not perfect. I'm not *fixed*. I'm not some polished storybook ending.

I'm a woman who was rescued—and now knows the Rescuer by name.

And if you've made it this far into my story, maybe you need to hear this too: It's not too late.

Not for you. Not for the one you love. Not for the child you lost to addiction. Not for the version of yourself you think is too far gone.

If there's breath in your lungs—there's hope.

I'm living proof. This is my story. But it's not the end. It's just the beginning.

I spent years looking for a hero. I didn't realize... I'd have to become the heroine of my own story.

www.ingramcontent.com/pod-product-compliance
Lightning Source LLC
Chambersburg PA
CBHW011220120626
46545CB00010B/3089